W9-CNA-131

Women of Achievement

Tina Fey

Women *of* Achievement

Abigail Adams
Susan B. Anthony
Tyra Banks
Clara Barton
Hillary Rodham Clinton
Marie Curie
Ellen DeGeneres
Diana, Princess of Wales
Tina Fey
Ruth Bader Ginsburg
Joan of Arc
Helen Keller
Madonna
Michelle Obama
Sandra Day O'Connor
Georgia O'Keeffe
Nancy Pelosi
Rachael Ray
Anita Roddick
Eleanor Roosevelt
Martha Stewart
Barbara Walters
Venus and Serena Williams

Women of *Achievement*

Tina Fey

WRITER AND ACTRESS

Janet Hubbard-Brown

CHELSEA HOUSE
P U B L I S H E R S
An imprint of Infobase Publishing

TINA FEY

Chelsea House
An imprint of Infobase Publishing
132 West 31st Street
New York, NY 10001

Library of Congress Cataloging-in-Publication Data
Hubbard-Brown, Janet.
 Tina Fey : writer and actress / Janet Hubbard-Brown.
 p. cm. — (Women of achievement)
 Includes bibliographical references and index.
 ISBN 978-1-60413-709-5 (hardcover)
 1. Fey, Tina, 1970– Juvenile literature. 2. Television actors and actresses—United States—Biography—Juvenile literature. 3. Women television writers—United States—Biography—Juvenile literature. 4. Women comedians—United States—Biography—Juvenile literature. 5. Women television producers and directors—United States—Biography—Juvenile literature. I. Title. II. Series.

PN2287.F4255H83 2010
791.4502'8092—dc22
[B]
                        2010001374

Text design by Erik Lindstrom
Cover design by Ben Peterson
Composition by EJB Publishing Services
Cover printed by Bang Printing, Brainerd, Minn.
Book printed and bound by Bang Printing, Brainerd, Minn.
Date printed: September 2010
Printed in the United States of America
10 9 8 7 6 5 4 3 2 1

This book is printed on acid-free paper.

CONTENTS

The Most Successful Woman in Comedy

On September 15, 2008, 38-year-old Tina Fey, looking fabulous in an eggplant strapless gown, her long brown hair dancing around her shoulders, received three Emmy Awards (the equivalent of the Academy Award for television actors) at the Nokia Theatre in Los Angeles: the first for the outstanding sitcom series she created in 2006, *30 Rock*, the second for her performance in that series, and a third for her writing on it. In an acceptance speech for one of the awards, she said, "I want to thank my parents for somehow raising me to have confidence that is disproportionate with my looks and abilities. . . . Well done—that is what all parents should do."[1]

In 2009, Fey won an Emmy for her impersonation of the 2008 Republican vice-presidential candidate, Sarah

Palin, on *Saturday Night Live* (*SNL*). Though Palin was then governor of Alaska, most Americans had never heard of the former beauty queen and mother of five with the wide smile, rimless glasses, beehive hairstyle, and high-pitched voice until presidential candidate Senator John McCain of Arizona asked her to be his running mate—the first time in the history of the Republican Party that a woman had been so honored.

Prior to her move into situation comedy, or sitcom, Fey—who bore an uncanny resemblance to Palin—had been the co-anchor of "Weekend Update" on *Saturday Night Live* from 2000 to 2006. After Sarah Palin hit the political circuit, Lorne Michaels, creator and producer of *Saturday Night Live*, asked Fey to return to the show and impersonate the candidate. Fey was initially resistant. But Michaels persisted, and when Fey's friend Amy Poehler agreed to join her in the skits, impersonating presidential candidate Hillary Clinton and anchorwoman Katie Couric, Fey said yes. Her brilliant impersonation of Palin on five shows proved to be an enormous hit. In fact, some were convinced that Fey's skewering of the election swayed it in favor of Senator Barack Obama of Illinois, the Democratic candidate. Fey dismissed such talk on the television show *The View*: "I like to think people are not swayed by sketch comedy. I hope they're a little smarter than that."[2]

A STEADY CLIMB TO THE TOP

Growing up, Tina Fey felt fortunate to have a mother who she thought was hilariously funny and a father and older brother who shared their love of sitcoms and comedy films with her. As she moved into adolescence, she used the humor she had learned at home to cover up her shyness. She had inherited her mother's biting wit, which manifested in her writing (she was on the high school newspaper staff) and in social groups. She worked at a local theater in

A publicity photo of Tina Fey for her television sitcom, *30 Rock*. The award-winning show, based on her experiences as a writer on *Saturday Night Live*, has been critically acclaimed since its debut in 2006.

summers, and then went off to the University of Virginia, where she majored in theater for four years. A hint of her determination to succeed became evident there—she took the same "Introduction to Theater" class four times. Also, though laughingly recalled as being "mousey" by one of her professors, she ended up with the lead in *Cabaret* her senior year, the first example of her ability to transform herself.

Chicago, known as a mecca for comedy, beckoned. She auditioned for The Training Center at Second City, where some of the greatest comedians performing had learned improvisation, a form of acting that requires complete spontaneity on the stage. She was rejected, but undaunted. She went to ImprovOlympic, where Del Close, who was considered a guru of improvisation, was teaching. (To support herself, she took a job at the YMCA, where she made $7 an hour folding towels.) A few months later she was accepted at her second audition for The Training Center. There, she studied under Martin de Maat, the artistic director who recognized her talent and used his influence to have her move up the hierarchy.

Scott Adsit, who was at Second City with her, and who is on her show *30 Rock*, recalled her as being mousey as well, but also brimming with talent and determination to succeed. In a stroke of luck, she was accepted onto the Mainstage, and once there, she really began to prove herself. Through a friend, Adam McKay, who had left Second City and become head writer at *Saturday Night Live*, she submitted sketches to producer Lorne Michaels. He invited her to come to New York and work on the show. Michaels was seeking a writer with a female sensibility. As was the case at Second City, male writers and comics far outnumbered women, which meant that the humor had been more rowdy/male from the start.

Fey's physical transformation on *SNL* has been well documented. Maureen Dowd wrote in *Vanity Fair*:

> Elizabeth Stamatina Fey started as a writer and per-
> former with a bad short haircut in Chicago improv.
> Then she retreated backstage at *SNL*, wore a ski hat,
> and gained weight writing sharp, funny jokes and
> eating junk food. Then she lost 30 pounds, fixed her
> hair, put on a pair of hot-teacher glasses.[3]

In 2000, after three years as a writer on the show, Fey was made head writer, a position which put her in charge of the staff writers, and in that same year she became the first female co-anchor of "Weekend Update" since the late 1970s. Wearing a blue blazer and glasses that became her trademark, she wowed audiences with her one-liners and biting wit.

CHANGING THE FACE OF TELEVISION COMEDY

Fey often talks about her life in relation to her work, and much of her work relates to her life. For example, after her film *Mean Girls* opened in 2004, she admitted to ridiculing "wayward classmates, reserving particular scorn for kids who drank, cut school, overdressed, or slept around."[4] For *30 Rock*, she created a character named Liz Lemon, whose life is based on the seven years Fey spent on *SNL* as head writer.

Fey's experiences have been instrumental in changing the face of television comedy with her show *30 Rock*, a fictional sketch comedy show. Nancy Franklin wrote in the *New Yorker*, "*30 Rock* doesn't have the neat structure of most sitcoms; its roots are in sketch comedy and in improv, with their set pieces and their eagerness to keep you entertained every second without worrying too much about the story."[5] *New York Times* writer Ross Simonini explained that "the digressions themselves are what give the characters meaning and the show its substance."[6] He also believed that *30 Rock* is "a bold experiment in

In addition to working on television, Tina Fey has found success writing for and starring in films. Here, she is seen with Rob Lowe in *The Invention of Lying*, a 2009 comedy directed by Ricky Gervais and Matthew Robinson.

narrative."[7] Fans appreciate the ironic (stating the opposite of the truth in order to make people laugh) and deadpan humor that Fey is now famous for.

NO TIME TO BASK

By the time Fey was handed her Emmy in September 2009 for impersonating Sarah Palin, she had accumulated six Emmy awards, four Writers Guild of America awards, three Golden Globe awards, and three Screen Actors Guild awards. She had changed her image from ugly duckling to being voted one of their "50 Most Beautiful People" in 2003 by the editors of *People*. She had been featured on the covers of *Vanity Fair*, *Entertainment Weekly*, *Parade*, *Current Biography*, and *Harper's Bazaar*. In 2008, she was listed as "One of the 100 People Who Shape Our World" by *Time* and was among the 50 "Creativity 50" presented by *Creativity Magazine*. In 2009, she was named a "Wonder Woman"—perfectly wonderful and worthy of admiration—by the editors of *Town & Country*.

Not a hint of scandal has ever been associated with Fey. No stories of infidelity or crazy tantrums exist. She has never been involved in drugs or partying, and today it is a point of pride for her. She likes being a role model for teens. It is tempting to imagine someone at the peak of fame standing back and basking in the glory, but it is doubtful that Fey has the time to look back. She has a book to write, for which she was offered a $5 million advance. She continues to write and perform for *30 Rock* and has recently starred in a pair of new films: *The Invention of Lying* (2009) and *Date Night* (2010). Aside from all of her creative work, Fey manages to carve out time to spend with her daughter, Alice Zenobia, and husband, Jeff Richmond, and remains close to her parents and brother.

To her fans, Fey represents what is best about America—the strong work ethic, the success achieved through hard work, loyalty to family and friends, a refusal to succumb to the more shallow aspects of stardom. More than America's sweetheart, which Fey was called in *Vanity Fair*, she stands as the embodiment of the American dream.

A Talented Geek

Elizabeth Stamatina Fey was welcomed into the world on May 18, 1970, in Upper Darby, Pennsylvania, by her parents, Zenobia "Jeanne" and Donald Fey (a university grant proposal writer), and by her brother, Peter. Her mother was Greek; her father's family was of German and Scottish descent. In interviews, Tina has referred to herself as a "mystery ethnic." "The Greek kids would be like, 'You know she's Greek,' because I was passing. I was the Lena Horne of the Greek community."[1] (Lena Horne was a light-skinned African-American singer.)

From an early age, Tina was introduced to comedy. Her parents snuck her in to see *Young Frankenstein*. A great night lineup on television, in her mind, was "Mary Tyler Moore into Bob Newhart into Carol Burnett."[2] She said, "My dad has a good sense of silliness. He was the one to let me and my brother stay up to watch *Monty Python's Flying Circus*. He introduced us to the Marx Brothers, Laurel and Hardy and even *The Three Stooges*."[3] She also liked watching *An Evening at the Improv* and *The Honeymooners*. *SCTV* (*Second City TV*, filmed in Toronto, Canada), which was picked up by NBC, was also a favorite of the Fey family in the late 1970s. Peter, eight years older than Tina, stayed up and watched *Saturday Night Live* and often acted out the skits for her the next day.

Fey claims her biting wit comes from her mother: "My mom is very, very dry. If she's out and sees a woman in a reaeeeeally ugly hat, or a crazy ugly Christmas sweater, my mom will go out of her way to be like: 'I love your sweater! That is be-autiful. Where did you get it?'"[4] In fact, the family often did comedy routines around the table. According to her brother, Peter, Tina had a unique sense of humor: "When she was about seven, she drew this street scene of people walking along, holding hands with huge chunks of Camembert and Cheddar. At the bottom she wrote, 'What a friend we have in cheeses!'"[5]

WONDERFUL PARENTS

When Tina was five, a man slashed her cheek with a knife. Years later, her husband, Jeff Richmond, explained the mystery of her scar to an interviewer at *Vanity Fair*: "It was in . . . the front yard of her house, and somebody just came up, and she just thought somebody marked her with a pen."[6] Fey said later, "It's a childhood injury that was kind of grim. And it kind of bums my parents out for me to talk about it."[7]

While the experience was undoubtedly traumatizing for the entire family, Fey maintains that in spite of it she was a confident little girl and attributes that quality to her parents. She said:

The rising Comcast Center skyscraper *(top center left)* is shown among other skyscrapers in Philadelphia. In the foreground is Upper Darby, Pennsylvania, Tina Fey's hometown.

My parents were extremely supportive and always made it seem like we could achieve anything we wanted. They were generous with their praise and their time but also good, strict parents. The first time one of my friends met them, my mom came in and gave me a million kisses. My friend was like, "I don't even know what that is. I don't understand parents like that." It always just felt like there was a real safety net there. It made it okay to try.[8]

A profile emerges of a little girl who was the darling of her parents' eyes, quite funny at home but shy and introverted at school. She said, "I was more of the weird kid who came home after school, put on my colonial-lady costume from Halloween and did little skits for myself."[9] She claimed she would say "smart-mouth things around the house so my parents would laugh, and I would keep doing it and sometimes I would be a little too smart-mouthed and get into trouble. So very early on I was trying to figure out how to walk that line, how to be funny without necessarily being offensive."[10]

SCHOOL DAYS

As a student Tina attended Cardington Elementary School and Beverly Hills Middle School. As early as eighth grade, she wrote an independent study program on the nature of comedy. The only book she could find on comedy was *Encyclopedia of Comedy* by Joe Franklin. She had already determined on her own that she "may not be super-pretty. This comedy thing may be my best move."[11] She had learned, as many comedians had before her, that being funny was the perfect foil for shyness.

When asked if she was a miserable, insecure kid, Fey replied, "No, I was a mostly happy child, though I had a pretty rough puberty. Growing up as a girl is always traumatizing. . . . But I think it's good to grow up that way. It builds character."[12]

In another interview, she recalled:

Somewhere around the fifth or seventh grade I figured out that I could ingratiate myself to people by making them laugh. Essentially, I was just trying to make them like me. But after a while it became a part of my identity. I remember at the end of the year in my eighth grade algebra class, I wrote a note to the teacher that basically said, "I know that I'm kinda a cutup and I like to crack the jokes now and again, but it's only because I struggle with math."[13]

DID YOU KNOW?

Tina Fey has a faint scar that lines the left side of her face. When she was five, she was playing in her front yard when a stranger approached her and slashed her cheek. "She just thought somebody slashed her with a pen," her husband, Jeff Richmond, said in an interview in the January 2009 issue of *Vanity Fair*. He said that it was fascinating to him.

This is somebody who, no matter what it was, has gone through something. And I think it really informs the way she thinks about her life. When you have that kind of thing happen to you, that makes you scared of certain things . . . your comedy comes out in a different kind of way, and it also makes you feel for people.

Did she feel less attractive growing up because of it? Fey said, "I don't think so. . . . Because I proceeded unaware of it. I was a very confident little kid. It's really almost like I'm kind of

In a 2003 interview, Fey said that at Upper Darby High School she was "playing offense a little bit. Like to a guy friend, I'd say, 'Really? That's who you like?' I would try to control people through shame. I only learned how to stop doing that like two years ago."[14] She was by no stretch of the imagination a part of the "cool" kids, and in fact disapproved of the drug use and drinking that were going on. She had a few English teachers who encouraged her with her writing. She wrote a column for *The Acorn*, her school newspaper, giving herself the pen name of "The Colonel." It was a subversive column, in which she made fun of rigid teachers and school policies. Frustratingly, the writer remained anonymous—for years!

????????????????????????

able to forget about it, until I was on-camera, and it became a thing of 'Oh, I guess we should use this side' or whatever."

In 2001, after the terrorist attacks of 9/11 and the announcement soon after that the poison anthrax had been delivered to news anchor Tom Brokaw, Fey left the NBC studio and did not return for hours because she was in such a state of high anxiety. She decided to get therapy to help her through it, as her extreme reaction, she knew, had to do with the violent attack on her when she was five. When asked her how the childhood attack affected her as a mother, she replied, "Supposedly, I will go crazy. My therapist says, 'When Alice is the age that you were, you may go crazy.' She said, 'It's impossible to talk about it without somehow seemingly exploiting it, and glorifying it.'"*

* Maureen Dowd, "What Tina Wants," *Vanity Fair*, January 2009, p. 72.

Marlene Kimble, Fey's best friend from Upper Darby, described how they liked to "hang out in her mother's kitchen and eat chocolate cake and play Scrabble."[15] Tina was in a group referred to as the "AP-class brainiac nerds."[16] She sang in the chorus and edited the high school paper. She did not date. She said, "I was a very good kid. I went to college. I didn't drink, didn't smoke, didn't do drugs. Comedy was the one place I was able to misbehave."[17] Asked if she sees her humor as a gift, she said, "Every kid has something they're good at, that you hope they find and gravitate toward."[18]

SUMMER THEATER

Harry Dietzler, who has run the Summer Stage for 35 years and who directed shows at Upper Darby High School when Tina Fey was there, recalled her being "quiet and shy, but very clever. She made funny behind-her-hands comments and people would snicker."[19]

At Fey's high school, he directed *Grease*, in which she played the part of Frenchy. He recalled her singing "Adelaide's Lament" in a show that he staged called *Show Stoppers*. She took on the serious role of Dr. Van Helsing in *Dracula* one year. In her senior year, she directed *The Little Mermaid*. One Tuesday morning she wrapped the show, and on Tuesday afternoon held auditions for her next show, the Hans Christian Andersen story *The Ugly Duckling*. One day she came to Dietzler in tears because her actors were switching over to a more popular show. He said, "I stepped in and made all those cast in Tina's show return."[20]

She and a friend, Jane Baker, were good at improvisation even then. Dietzler said that they would put on a show based on *Whose Line Is It Anyway?* between rehearsals one summer. "They made up incredibly funny scenes,"[21] he said.

Tina Fey's senior year high school yearbook photo from Upper Darby High School in Pennsylvania, in 1988. Her love of performing and comedy was apparent even then.

When Fey returned to her hometown with Katie Couric in 2004, the entire community was in a state of excitement. Dietzler said that the identity of "The Colonel," the column that appeared in the high school newspaper, *The Acorn*, all those years ago, had continued to remain a secret. When Katie Couric was told about it, she asked Fey if she was indeed "The Colonel." Fey said yes, and the issue was finally laid to rest.

OFF TO COLLEGE

Fey went to the University of Virginia as an English major. "I loved it there," she said. "It was such a foreign atmosphere to me, so Southern and genteel. After my neighborhood, that was hilarious to me, just to see that many blondes."[22] The university, founded by Thomas Jefferson and boasting one of the most beautiful campuses in the country, had a country-club atmosphere. Fey said in an interview that her mother was not sent to college because it was not what was expected of girls in her family. When Fey was accepted at UVA, her mother took an extra job in order to afford the tuition.

One of Fey's professors, Douglas Grissom, who continues to teach playwriting and also teaches a general appreciation course called "Introduction to Theater," said, "Tina probably took it four times."[23] At the time he wondered if she had any idea of going into theater. (She did, in fact, switch her major to theater.)

When asked what she was like as a student, Grissom thought for a moment before responding. He said, "She was a quiet, demure little girl. She was not stunning looking. Sort of average. Very personable. She had a great smile."[24] When asked about the scar on her face, he said that it was more noticeable then than it is now. He added, "She was a charming person you always enjoyed seeing. She was not mean-spirited and had a sharp sense of humor."[25]

He recognized her talent early on. She was in another of his writing classes, which involved independent study, and he recalled that some of her early scenes were memorable. "We also had a graduate writing program," he said, "and she became part of our graduate workshop though she was still an undergraduate. She held her own."[26] His method of teaching was to "learn by doing." He would give out specific writing exercises, one of which was to write a 10-page scene. The students would read their scenes out loud in class and critique one another's work. He recalled one of Fey's short plays called "Sunday Girls," which was about having a sleepover. Though it was primarily funny, Grissom recalled that "she had some serious issues that she dealt with in poetic moments."[27]

Like most university theater departments, the syllabus required that the students spend a lot of time working on productions. There were typically more girls in the theater department than boys, but it was more evenly divided in the playwriting class. He said, "Tina was definitely a vibrant member of the department. She worked in the box office and the costume shop like everyone else, and she was very enthusiastic about other people's work, other writers. She would tell them she loved their work."[28]

Each summer Fey would return to Summer Stage and either direct or work in the box office. One summer she was the publicity director, but did little performing. At the end of four years, Grissom definitely noticed a transformation in her. "She started out on the periphery," he said, "and ended up playing the lead role of Sally Bowles in *Cabaret*."[29] It was a tremendous leap for her as a performer.

In an interview conducted with the author on October 18, 2009, Tina's acting professor Richard Warner noted that the professors in the drama school were all professionals and described the University of Virginia itself as "very egalitarian, not really a southern town, and very social."[30]

He added, "UVA students are very bright, very warm. We are a polyglot community. We like to say we are 70 percent academic, and 30 percent social."[31] Then he laughed. "She's [Tina's] a good wa-hoo [an affectionate name for UVA graduates]," he said. "A wa-hoo," he added, "is a species of fish that can consume large amounts of liquid."[32] (He was no doubt referring to the school's reputation for being a party school, perhaps not realizing that Tina was a teetotaler.)

He spoke about his first impression of Tina. "She was in three of my acting classes," he said. "What struck me was her bright eyes, looking up at you. Hmm, I thought, who's this? She would say things so accurately right at the right time, and she was very good at listening. She was very shy, but there was always that gaze."[33]

Later in the interview he recalled how she looked in those days. "Physically, she was petite," he said. "A bit mousey. A little adult for her time. . . . When she did doll up, everyone would compliment her and she would say, 'Stop it.' She tried to hide herself from being seen onstage. I worked to make her visible. 'Take stage, take stage!' I would say over and over. She was reluctant. She had to learn that."[34]

During the interview, his memories of her seemed to flood back. Warner recalled:

> Her one lead role was Sally Bowles in *Cabaret*. She did a lot of supporting roles over the years. We had these little lab scenes then on Friday afternoons. Invariably she had written something. I'd literally take off my glasses and weep with laughter! She would take gossip and ramp it! The faculty got plenty of zingers.[35]

Warner also remembered another time when he created exercises in his class to have the students work with emotions. One of those was to have them put their hands in a pleading gesture, then bring them together saying, "Hold me, hold me." The next day, he said:

> I arrived at my desk and there was a little plastic animal in the center of my desk with a tiny bubble note attached that said, *Hold me!* Tina had gone somewhere and found that and created the joke. That was her communicating to me, "I'm not sure of this activity."[36]

Another story came up. It was Tina's final year and as director, Warner had selected a World War II play with an all-male cast. "She let me know that this was *not* a good idea," he said. "She and a girlfriend of hers were kind of angry."[37] Warner was ready to cast the play when he learned that two other actors wanted to audition. He said, "Tina and this girl walked in wearing full army gear, including helmets. They did this whole big Army thing and just left."[38] He paused, then added, "In other words, she takes the extra mile."[39]

It was he who suggested that Tina go to graduate school in Chicago, and when she discovered that that was not the answer for her and called him for advice, he told her to try improvisation. The rest is history.

Training Ground for Comedy

In 1948, a famous Chicago writer, A.J. Liebling, wrote an article about his city in the *New Yorker*, referring to it as "the second city." Three men—Paul Sills, Bernard Sahlins, and Howard Alk—who started a theater in Chicago in 1959 latched onto the name, The Second City, as the name for their theater group. Their goal was to teach an improvisation style created by Sills' mother, Violo Spolin.

Charna Halpern, who started another theater called ImprovOlympic (IO) in 1981, wrote that improvisation is simply "getting onstage and performing without any preparation or planning."[1] Some actors have compared it to freefalling. Jane Morris, who was at Second City from the late 1970s to 1989, said that improvisation is "a uniquely American art form, just as musical theater is."[2] The revues produced at Second City incorporated sarcasm, irony, and ridicule as a means of creating brilliant satire.

The form attracted people who were looking for something new. Actor Alan Arkin wrote about the earliest days of Second City, "My sense of the actors in the early years was that we were a diverse and multi-talented bunch of misfits. We all had broad interests and abilities, but no real specialties. We had nowhere else to go. We were saving our lives by being at Second City."[3]

IMPROVISATION

Improvisation proved to be a revelation for Fey. In an interview with Oprah Winfrey, she said:

> Serious acting was not really quite what I was intended for. When I studied acting technique, I could never understand what I should be thinking about when I was onstage. I'd be standing and thinking, "Hmmm, how does my hair look?" But with improv, the focus is clear: you're supposed to be listening to the other person so you know how to respond.[4]

Fey caught on quickly that the performer had to seek connections in a scene. In other words, the line that is spoken after someone else's has to be inspired by what is happening on the stage in that moment. The mind is not allowed to wander for even a split second, for the performer must remember each idea that is suggested and incorporate it back into their scenes.

Craig Cackowski, who spent years learning and teaching improv, named the qualities one needed in order to succeed in improvisation. He listed patience, then added, "There's a lot of improv that is just waiting for the right time and knowing the right time and not rushing things. Listening is . . . obviously number one, two and three."[5] He thinks it is important to keep it simple, "not trying to conquer the world with a scene . . . recognizing the game when it happens, creating patterns and following those patterns and respecting them . . . and just having the right feel for give and take."[6]

Improvisation was also about learning how to fail. Alan Arkin said, "There is no place to fail anymore. And failing at something is crucial. We knew [at Second City] that 20, 30, sometimes 40 percent of what we were doing wasn't going to work. The audience didn't mind."[7]

ACQUIRING A NATIONAL REPUTATION

In 1975, when Lorne Michaels created *Saturday Night Live*, the late-night sketch comedy show broadcast out of New York City, he sought talent from Second City. Early *SNL* cast members John Belushi, Dan Aykroyd, Bill Murray, and Gilda Radner were among the first Second City performers to head to New York to achieve stardom. The founders of Second City also established a Second City in Toronto, which first featured talents like Mike Myers and Catherine O'Hara, who eventually migrated to Second City Chicago, a stepping-stone to *SNL* for the super talented.

How important were Second City alumni to comedy on film and television in the 1980s? A few notable examples include the 1984 hit film *Ghostbusters*, which was written by Dan Aykroyd and Harold Ramis, and starred Aykroyd, Ramis, and Bill Murray. Shelley Long and George Wendt, who also trained at Second City, were featured in the long-running sitcom *Cheers*, and Betty Thomas became a regular on *Hill Street Blues*.

In 1985, *Time* hailed Second City the "capital of comedy."[8] Improvisation, in fact, had become so popular that the Second City founders started a training center in

The awning-covered entrance to The Second City comedy club in Chicago, where Tina Fey and many other future *Saturday Night Live* stars got their starts.

Chicago, where a new generation of comedians including Mike Myers, Steve Carell, Stephen Colbert, and Chris Farley all continued on to national success.

HOW THE SYSTEM WORKED

When actress Jane Morris arrived at Second City in 1970, there was the Mainstage and the Touring Company, referred to as Tour Co. by actors. She spoke about the process of making it to Mainstage, which was, and still remains, the ultimate destination. She said, "We auditioned for Bernie Sahlins and producer Joyce Sloan, who required us to perform five different characters in five minutes. It was referred to as 'five through the door.'"[9]

The touring company, of which Morris was a longtime member, went to Chateau Louise, located in a distant suburb of Chicago. She explained that at that time the actors maintained the same grueling schedule as the Mainstage performers: eight performances a week, with the theater closed only on Christmas Day and Tuesdays. What was different at the touring company was that performers were not allowed to deliver original material, but were required to perform what had already been created on the Mainstage.

From the beginning, there were five men and two women on a Mainstage team. Morris explained, "There was a fat guy, a blue collar guy, a smart guy, and a clown for the men, and for the two women, there was a pretty woman and a not-pretty woman. That was the formula."[10] She paused. "I was the not-pretty woman."[11] She knew fairly early on that it would be unlikely that she would make it to Mainstage, for though she was considered exceptionally funny, one of the cofounders, Bernie Sahlins, did not like her. Furthermore, neither Sahlins nor Del Close, a prominent teacher, thought women were funny. There was the added factor, Morris said, that you "had to wait for someone to die before you got your turn on Mainstage."[12]

Morris and Jeff Michalski, a director, were one of approximately 30 couples who met at Second City and later married. (Tina Fey and Jeff Richmond would be among them in 2001.) Morris and Michalski, along with

Tina Fey and her husband, Jeff Richmond, arrive at a screening of *Anchorman: The Legend of Ron Burgundy* at the Museum of Television and Radio in New York City, on July 7, 2004. The couple met as fellow Second City performers.

Bill Applebaum and Jim Fay, formed a rebellious group in 1982. They were chomping at the bit to do their own material; with the approval of producer Joyce Sloane, and without the knowledge of Bernie Sahlins, they created an original revue, *Cows on Ice*, that was a smash hit. It was the start of E.T.C. Stage, the theater where most of the actors would train after they finished the touring company leg of the journey to the big stage.

TWO EXTRAORDINARY TEACHERS

Two teachers at Second City acquired guru status in the world of improvisation: Martin de Maat and Del Close, who were completely different in style and temperament. Both men had their loyal followers, and both would find Tina Fey special. Martin de Maat, a sensitive, nurturing man, had taken over as director of the Training Center at Second City from Del Close. Del Close was bigger than life, intimidating, and brilliant. Drugs and alcohol were his demons, and he went through firings from Second City, tried rehabilitation several times, and finally ended up in a partnership with a woman named Charna Halpern after leaving Second City for good in 1983. They created a separate improvisation theater, ImprovOlympic, where they would teach the long form of improvisation called "the Harold" that Close had started using in the 1960s.

In comparing the two methods taught at the two theaters, George Wendt said, "To me, taking a theme and working on your feet—without discussions, qualifications, setups, blackouts, and the like—is a much purer and easier way to find kernels of scenes that could be expanded and written."[13] He compared it to the Second City way, which was to "take a bunch of suggestions and write them on a piece of paper, stand backstage in the Green Room, and stare at a blackboard with a bunch of suggestions on it."[14]

A NEW ERA AT SECOND CITY

In the early 1990s, another wave of students entered Chicago; among them were Tina Fey, Jack McBrayer, and Amy Poehler. By that time Second City had turned into a huge commercial enterprise under owner Andrew Alexander, who had purchased the theater in 1985 after creating the successful Second City in Toronto. He was described by Mike Thomas in his book *The Second City Unscripted* as a "wealthy, well-coiffed, aloof-seeming interloper."[15] He was not popular.

He worked to create a better system for casting for the three touring companies—RedCo, BlueCo, and GreenCo. Resident companies were Second City, E.T.C. Stage Second City Northwest (in another suburb of Chicago), Second City Toronto, and Second City Detroit. The Training Center, which had opened in 1985, was by the early 1990s attracting thousands of students each year and making big profits for the organization. In the late 1980s, Alexander, wanting to expand to Los Angeles, managed to form a partnership with Ron Howard and Brian Grazer, two successful film directors. Morris and Michalski were in the first group to go west. She said, "[Alexander] wanted to have a television/film production factory running out of Second City. Like, any scene you did could be a potential sitcom. And so we actually did a lot of pitches and meetings and stuff. It was horrible."[16] The concept failed, and Alexander returned to Chicago. In 1990, he started a Business Theatre wing, which was geared toward workshops and shows for local corporations.

There were other problems in Chicago as well. The sight lines in the new theater were terrible, the show was not getting laughs, and young audiences were not showing up. There were major concerns that Second City had grown too fast and had too many touring companies. Some complained that it had become too institutional. There was also a strong hierarchy at work. When Sahlins retired, the atmosphere began to change, according to Morris. For the first time, directors were given more freedom. And Tina Fey was among the new wave of "hopefuls" to arrive in this new era.

FEY AUDITIONS

When Fey arrived in Chicago, three improv training centers were in operation: Second City, Players Workshop, and ImprovOlympic. Craig Cackowski arrived in Chicago from William and Mary College in Virginia at approximately the same time Fey did and began taking classes at Improv-Olympic. He explained what it was like there: There were

TWO INFLUENTIAL TEACHERS

Fey worked with Del Close at ImprovOlympic (IO). Close went to IO in 1985 after being fired several times from Second City, always returning. His reputation as a brilliant and difficult teacher and innovator continued to grow at IO, where he was able to focus on the long form of improvisation he had created called "the Harold." He was unkempt and grouchy, but mesmerizing. It was no secret that he was mentally unstable because of his addiction to alcohol and amphetamines. (He even lived for a while at a psychiatric hospital.) His passion was improvisation, and if he hated what he saw his actors doing, he let them know it. What he stressed over and over was that the work had to be honest, and this was instilled in Fey and her colleagues early on. He had declared many times that he did not think women were funny, but for reasons that are not clear, he decided that Fey and Poehler were funny. The day before he died he held a party in his hospital room, and many old friends came to pay their last respects.

8 teams, and 12 performers on his team. The introductory teacher was Charna Halpern, and Level 3 was taught by Del Close. The theater was in a bar called Wrigleyside. Adam McKay, who would later become head writer at *Saturday Night Live*, came on as a coach, and at one point Tina Fey joined Cackowski's team.

Cackowski auditioned for Second City TourCo twice and was not accepted. He described those auditions as cattle calls, where the actor was given 15 minutes to do a conducted scene. He went back for a third audition, which

Martin de Maat could not have been more different from Close, and the two did not get along. De Maat came from a working-class family and rose up to the role of teacher at Second City. Jeff Rogers, who knew him well, said, "He was a singular individual. If there was a person built from love, that was the guy. Support and love came out of his pores."* When asked if de Maat was a special mentor to Fey, Rogers answered, "He mentored Tina, but he also mentored everyone else. His message was that we should work together as a team, and support each other blindly."**

When students did not get into the Training Center, he would sit down and talk to them. He believed that Fey had the talent and the drive to succeed and helped to move her along her path.

---

* Mike Thomas, *The Second City Unscripted: Revolution and Revelation at the World-Famous Comedy Theater*. New York: Random House, 2009.
** Author interview with Jeff Rogers, December 17, 2009.

was a closed audition. This time the 8 actors had 45 minutes to show what they could do and he was accepted. Jeff Rogers, who had started at Second City in 1989, said that the following staff members were in the room when he auditioned: Joyce Sloan, Joe Keith, Ron West, and Kelly Leonard. The improvisers were asked to do "three through the door" rather than the "five through the door" that Morris had performed. Rogers, who for a time was director of the Business Wing of Second City, explained in an interview with the author, "We were given a couple of games. We went up with a group of six to 10 people, and walked through a few improv games. They were watching to see how we played with others and what our instincts were."[17]

On the other hand, Cackowski and the other touring company actors had a script to work with, and they were allowed to do improv around it. They performed about 10 shows a month. He was moved up to E.T.C. Stage in 1998. (By that time Fey had left for *Saturday Night Live*.)

Another actor at Second City at the time got sick of the hierarchy and refused to follow the rules. Jeff Garlin, who left Second City to star in and executive produce *Curb Your Enthusiasm*, talked about the process of "making it" at Second City. He was there five years but refused to take classes, and then created friction because he wanted to be a regular cast member and was informed that he had to earn that privilege. He got angry and left. His parting words were, "Look, I'm outta here. . . . I'm going off to Hollywood shortly, and I'm gonna become a big success, and I'll end up hiring all of you."[18] He did exactly that. Today, he is listed on the Second City Web site as a famous alumnus.

FEY'S MOVEMENT UP THE LADDER

Fey said that the "first time I went to see a Second City show, I was in awe of everything. I just wanted to touch the same stage that Gilda Radner had walked on. It was sacred ground."[19] (Radner was one of the most popular women to perform both at Second City and on *SNL*. She died of ovarian cancer in 1989.) Fey was rejected when she first auditioned for Second City Training Center in 1993. She, like Cackowski, decided to train at ImprovOlympic.

To support herself, Fey lived in a rough neighborhood with a roommate and took a job at the Evanston YWCA, working the 5:30 A.M. to 2 P.M. shift, which meant she could take classes at Second City at night. In 1994, Fey met Jeff Richmond, nine years older and an inch shorter than she (she was five feet four and a half inches). She gave a hint of what it was like for them then. A bar near Wrigley Field was the IO base. She recalled:

[It] was a good space and had very good chicken fingers. Jeff Richmond, my husband, was the piano player at the time and he used to have to park his car by Wrigley Field either on a game night or in the middle of freezing cold winter, and then, like, haul two huge keyboards a few blocks, up the stairs to Wrigley Side, play for two Harold [long-form improvisation] shows, and then hurry and pack up all his stuff before the blues band went on. And then he made, like, $25.[20]

The next time Fey auditioned, she was accepted into the training program. She recalled in an interview:

It was a funny sort of pattern in the improv world— the girls were all these well-educated, nice, obedient girls and improv is some sort of outlet. Then there were a lot of guys who did two years of college or one year of college, they never finished and they liked to buck authority. So the reasons they're drawn to improv and sketch are the opposite.[21]

FEY CONSIDERED TALENTED

Morris said that with all the hierarchy and auditioning, if "someone comes in and blows the director away she will get in."[22] Rogers said that it was "relatively rare for someone to succeed as quickly as Fey did." She was not in the Training Center long when de Maat suggested that she move on to one of the touring companies. The goal of the directors, according to Rogers, "was to create ensembles that would work well together,"[23] and Fey proved a terrific team player. She was in the touring company for two years before being accepted to Mainstage in 1995. Fey recalled:

> I was very timid the first [rehearsal]. I didn't even really know how the process would work, and I remember [the director] would be trying to make coffee on the breaks, and I would go over to him and be like, [timid-sounding,] "Well, I think, maybe I had an idea we could do something." He'd be like, "Okay, tell it. In the rehearsal. Bring it up in rehearsal." And I'd be like, [timid voice,] "OK." And then I'd go back into rehearsal and not say anything. But eventually I sort of found my way in that company.[24]

The competition for stage time and membership in the more elite groups was fierce, but Fey and Amy Poehler, who were in class together, became fast friends. Scott Adsit, who performs with Fey on *30 Rock*, remembered her as being "a bit mousey in her big, puffy winter coat and these huge grandma hand-me-down glasses. But her ideas were great and she was a powerful member of the group pretty quickly."[25] Morris said, "In the Amy Poehler/Tina Fey equation, Amy Poehler was the pretty one, Fey the not-pretty one."[26]

Kelly Leonard, currently executive vice president of Second City, said:

Tina always did scenes on body issues, the feminine mystique. She was very attuned to what was different about women, especially in comedy, and she understood cruelty in a big way. I mean, she could cut people down big-time, and she's one of the nicest people I know.[27]

Jeff Richmond recalled, in a conversation with Virginia Heffernan, the first time he saw Fey doing improv at Second City. "I don't want to say she was funny 'for a woman,' but there were so many talented men there at the time, and then suddenly there was Tina, who was so funny—and she was at home with all those boys on the stage."[28] Sheldon Patinkin, who was a director there, recalled to *Chicago Tribune* reporter Steve Johnson that "[Steve] Carell and [Stephen] Colbert were star performers, Fey less so."[29] He explained, "Tina didn't stand out the way she does now. She was a victim, perhaps, of thinking more like a writer than a performer."[30]

CHANGES AT SECOND CITY

Jeff Rogers explains that sketch comedies are "situation or character-based short stories."[31] Fey would come to excel in this form. The old style of presenting sketches was feeling tired, and some rebels were coming in who were ready to buck the old system. Morris and Michalski's revues at E.T.C. Stage had paved the way for the arrival of director Mick Napier, who started Annoyance Theatre in Chicago after growing tired of the hierarchy and five levels of classes at Second City. According to Amy Seham, author of the book *Whose Improv Is It Anyway?*, his shows were "usually short on plot and long on eccentric characters, pop culture references, and opportunistic, ribald humor."[32]

Mick Napier came to direct a show called "Pinata Full of Bees," which was considered groundbreaking in that the people involved in it, including Adam McKay, Rachel Dratch, Mick Napier, and director Tom Gianas, were experimenting with a new style of creating scenes, and they were doing away with the older scene-blackout-scene-blackout method and eliminating themes. After *Variety* gave the show a good review, the original cast took it to Washington, D.C. to be performed at the Kennedy Center for the Performing Arts. *Saturday Night Live* producer Lorne Michaels saw it and ended up bringing Adam McKay and the director, Tom Gianas, to write for *SNL*.

FEY'S BIG BREAK

Fey's first big opportunity arrived in 1995 when Mick Napier asked her to replace Scott Glasier in "Pinata Full of Bees." She played all of his roles as written. In 1997, Napier cast the first equal-gender show in the history of Second City, "Paradigm Lost." Morris had created a show called "Channel This" at E.T.C. with more women than men (four women and three men) in 1989. When told to choose a number, the men would complain. "I need a girl," they would say. Morris would patiently explain, "You don't need a girl. You need a good improviser."[33] Napier said:

> I think that alone [an equally balanced cast] allowed women greater options on that stage, because they're no longer just the counterpart to a male, which is what a lot of scenes were. . . . There's this thing in the improv world on the Internet—endless discussions about how men treat women poorly in improvisation. . . . And Tina Fey or Amy Sedaris or Stephnie Weir would have never ever formed a

complaint about how men treated them onstage. What they would do instead is be wickedly . . . funny and strong and powerful with their choices on the stage. And be relatively silent otherwise.[34]

Aside from her natural talent for improvisation, Fey may have had some additional advantages over others vying for a spot on the Mainstage. One of the directors thought that the young were starting to come in with very little comedy knowledge. She suggested that they go home and watch old television comedies, shows that Fey, along with the rest of her family, had practically memorized. Another bonus was that she was respectful of others and was quick to offer praise, just as she had done at the University of Virginia. As in high school and at the University of Virginia, Fey was a disciplined and focused student, taking on more than was required. Her aversion to alcohol and drugs, which had caused too many in the Second City community to lose their way, was another plus. Her relationship with the older Jeff Richmond likely also provided stability.

GROWTH OF THEATER—AND TINA

Fey was on fire. In 1996, she, Rachel Dratch, and Jenna Jolovitz created a three-woman scene called "Citizen Gates," where they played politicians' wives coping with the political life. In the scene that made them standouts, Fey and Jolovitz played a lesbian couple who get a real-estate woman flustered when they show their emotional devotion to each other. Fey said that scene, and nightly sketches they did from suggestions from the audience, gave them the chance to show variety. Darel Jevens wrote in the *Chicago Sun-Times*, "Fey was able to develop one of her strongest characters—a tough-talking stripper—because she felt no need to resist a role that might seem stereotypical."[35]

After Fey was cast in *Paradigm Lost*, a reviewer called the show "one of the most original" and said it "has a higher level of first rate material than I can recall in any Second City production of the 1990s."[36] It was full of off-the-wall humor, developed as a flow of sketches instead of the usual assortment of skits and blackouts. Fey played a lesbian in one scene, a clerk at the YMCA folding laundry (a taste of reality), and an exotic dancer auditioning for a businessman. The reviewer went on to write:

> The revue, under Mick Napier's direction, never slackens in pace and the wild gear shifting in subject matter and mood keeps the audience alert and off balance. The entire cast of six is excellent, but I was particularly impressed with Fey, a new Mainstage performer to me, who has tremendous range as an actress. She scores equally well in manic characters and realistic figures, like a nurse patiently trying to draw blood from a frantically frightened donor.[37]

REJECTION

Fey told Virginia Heffernan at the *New Yorker*, "I'd had my eye on the show [*SNL*] forever, the way other kids have their eye on [New York Yankees shortstop] Derek Jeter."[38] In an interview with Oprah Winfrey, Fey was asked if people at Second City know when an *SNL* scout is coming, and her reply was "Oh, yes—like puppies in a pound: 'Take me, take me, take me!'"[39] *SNL* sent scouts to see the shows at Second City, but Fey was not invited to New York. She said, "My friend Adam McKay was already working at *SNL*, so I called him. That's how I eventually got a writing job there."[40]

Having written and performed in only two Second City Mainstage shows, she drafted several scripts to McKay, who liked them and showed them to producer Lorne Michaels. She then went to New York for an interview and Michaels hired her. She had six days to show up for work. She was 27 years old. Fey told Jancee Dunn of *Reader's Digest* that she started crying when she heard she had the *SNL* job. When the women from Second City took her out to dinner to celebrate, she said she had to get up from the table to vomit from pure nerves. "I've never had that before in my life,"[41] she added. In New York, she eventually found a walk-up apartment on the Upper West Side. Jeff Richmond would not join her there for another three years.

Working on *SNL* was not a guarantee of success. For many Second City alumni, the pressure to perform often led to tragic ends. Chris Farley, for example, died tragically in 1997. Overweight and addicted to alcohol and drugs, he had attended the annual holiday party at Second City and the next day he was dead. John Belushi had died from a drug overdose in 1982, and John Candy was found dead from a heart attack in 1994. Following these tragedies, Second City staff became "less tolerant—of bad behavior, of actor-audience scuffles, of chemically impaired performances, of anger mismanagement. Good for business? Yes. But some thought the housecleaning also scrubbed away the theater's rebel soul."[42]

Fey said she could have stayed at Second City, doing the eight shows a week, for years had she not been handed the opportunity at *Saturday Night Live*. Cast member Peter Grosz said:

> Sue Gillan [a cast mate] told me something amazing. She said Second City forces you to really be the person you are. You're put through some tests with other people, you have to question who you are, you have to create something. . . . And who everybody is really comes out, because while the stakes aren't that high, the amount of stuff you have to do is very personal and very interactive and it really runs the whole gamut of your personality.[43]

Success at
Saturday Night Live

When Tina Fey decided to leave Chicago for *Saturday Night Live* in New York, she began packing up her things. She said:

> I found an orange folder—a regular school folder—in a bookshelf. As soon as I saw it, I knew what it was. There were quotes written all over the front of it. Some of them were: "Greet everything with 'Yes, and. . .'" "Make statements instead of putting the burden on others with questions." "Stay in the present, as opposed to focusing on the past or future." "The fun is always on the other side of a yes."[1]

What she had written down were some of Martin de Maat's rules of improv. She said, "I realized that taking that class had completely changed my life."[2] She realized that she lived her life according to those rules, especially saying yes. "Say yes, and you'll figure it out afterward,"[3] for example, helped her to be more adventurous. "It has definitely helped me to be less afraid," she said. "Life is improvisation. All of those classes were like church to me. The training had seeped into me and changed who I am."[5]

A DIFFERENT WORLD

In 1997, when Fey started writing for *SNL*, there was a group of recurring characters—Will Ferrell as the high school cheerleader and Chris Kattan's Mango—that she knew not to interfere with. The show had 20 full-time writers, three of whom were women. Writers gathered on Monday morning to pitch ideas for the following week's show. Sketches were written by Tuesday night. By Wednesday, 40 skits were presented at the read-through, out of which 10 would be used. Fey worked hard to have her work be among them. Eventually her biting, satirical humor drew enough laughs that she became an accepted part of the group.

Of the then 15 regular cast members, all were expected to write. Generally, the cast came from one of three comedy farm teams: Second City, which included Rachel Dratch, Amy Poehler, and Tina Fey. Another group came from the Groundlings (Will Ferrell, Chris Farley, Maya Rudolph) in Los Angeles, who were known for their eccentric characters. The third group, which included Conan O'Brien, hailed from the *Harvard Lampoon*.

Because everyone knew the show was filmed live, writers/performers had to be on top of current events, but in fact, around the time Fey arrived, America was turning into a celebrity culture. Fey said that the show "was simply reflecting celebrity's domination of the national consciousness."[5] She admitted that doing gossipy celebrity send-ups helped to preserve her staff writing position. "If you look back at them, they do not hold up," she said. "But at the time, I was like, 'I got something on!' It was my first year, and I needed to figure out how to stay afloat."[6]

Saturday Night Live had always depended on guest hosts to enliven the show. Steve Martin, for example, could be depended on to carry a show, but many of the newer hosts were not good at comedy. Adam McKay noted, "*SNL* is only as good as its guest hosts."[7] He remembered as a kid seeing someone like Elvis Costello as host, and "you could tell everyone thought he was cool, and you were trying to figure out why. The show should be a little cooler than its audience," he said, "and when it goes into that Justin Timberlake–land, it becomes less cool."[8] Producer Lorne Michaels has a different view. He said, "I've always been, when in doubt, go young. Because lots of things are much more forgivable when it's someone young trying it."[9]

PROMOTION TO SUPERVISING WRITER

For two years, Fey was a sketch writer, and the only giveaway of the stress of her job was her weight gain. In 1999, Michaels offered her the position of head writer, making her the first woman in SNL history to be so honored. In interviews, she downplayed the significance. The media, however, saw

IN HER OWN WORDS

Unlike many female comics, Tina Fey believes that one does not have to be wacky to be funny. She once remarked:

> I think it's important to know you don't have to be insane to be creative, especially for women. You don't have to be nuts.

it as an indication of a changing comedy world. While she brought moral authority to the set, according to Virginia Heffernan of the *New Yorker*, "she has also made the show more lewd. . . . Jokes have also become more graphic."[10]

By 2003, Fey was writing two comedy sketches each week, and also running one of the two "rewrite" tables on Thursdays, where a few key people decided which sketches would run and which writers would get to join the staff. Nancy Franklin, in an article written for the *New Yorker*, stated that Fey's personal character had a great deal to do with her success as head writer. She mentioned Fey's tribute to her parents at the 2008 Emmy Awards ceremony, when she thanked them for raising her to be confident. Franklin wrote:

> That statement captured a little something of Fey's kind of humor and what one guesses (because one, not knowing her, doesn't know for sure) is a decency and a generosity that served her well when she became the first female head writer at *Saturday Night Live* in 1999, and had to manage a mostly male staff.[11]

In their book, *Live from New York*, Shales and Miller noted that *SNL* had female writers from its inception and its cast in the 1990s had a number of talented women. Janeane Garofalo, who finally quit, said, "Life is a boys club. So *SNL* is a reflection of that. But Molly Shannon and Ana Gasteyer and Cheri Oteri and Rachel Dratch and Tina Fey . . . came in and would not be denied."[12] She went on to point out that "she [Molly Shannon] is writing and writing and writing. . . . No gossiping, no nothing. . . . She didn't get involved with drugs and alcohol. She was there to work."[13] The same could be said of Fey, who in interviews described *SNL* as being like high school, but she has also defended the show, and Lorne Michaels in particular, because he gives tremendous freedom to his writers.

THE ACTOR TINA

In 2008, Oprah Winfrey asked Fey if she missed performing on *SNL* when she was just writing for the show, and she replied, "A little. At *SNL*, there are lots of frustrated performers working as writers. Lorne often turns actors into writers, and he's smart to do it. . . . But it's a little heartbreaking to be at *SNL* and not be on the air."[14]

Sue Mengers, a Hollywood agent known for her toughness, told Michaels that he could not put Fey in front of the camera. "She doesn't have the looks,"[15] she told him. Since she had started at *SNL*, Fey had added a lot of weight to her small frame, and the camera adds at least 10 pounds. By show business standards, Fey was already considered slightly heavy when she arrived, though her husband described her as having the kind of rounded figure that the artist Peter Paul Reubens might have liked to paint. Ultimately, Fey decided to join Weight Watchers and over several months she lost 30 to 35 pounds. A producer at *SNL*, Steve Higgins, recalled her famous makeover. "How did she go from ugly duckling into swan?" he asked. "She has such a German work ethic even though she's half Greek. It's superhuman, the German thing of 'This will happen and I am going to make this happen.' It's just sheer force of will."[16]

Fey joked about her image prior to losing weight. There was an additional legacy: "Because of the Greek-girl thing, I have, like, boobs and butt," so "I only have two speeds—either matronly or a little too slutty."[17] Another moniker was soon added to the young woman who had often been referred to as mousy: *sexy.*

DRATCH & FEY

Although Fey understood that she had been hired as a writer at *SNL*, she did miss performing. She continued to go on auditions, but never booked anything. She said, "I never booked commercials and I never got two lines on

Tina Fey and Rachel Dratch attend a benefit at the American Museum of Natural History in New York City in 2005. The good friends and fellow performers put on a two-woman show in 1999 called *Dratch & Fey* that made a big impression on Lorne Michaels, creator of *Saturday Night Live*.

Early Edition—nothing."[18] In 1999, her old friend Rachel Dratch called from Los Angeles to see if she wanted to put together a show. Dratch was at loose ends, unsure where to go next. Fey missed performing. They agreed to do a show, which they called *Dratch & Fey*. Richmond agreed to direct. In two weeks, they had put together a two-woman revue. It made a big splash in 1999, first in Chicago, then in New York.

Michaels went to see it in New York and made the decision to give Fey the plum spot of appearing as co-anchor of the six-minute "Weekend Update" fake news report on *SNL*. At first, Fey was unsure about doing it. Michaels talked her into it, which established a pattern whereby she would doubt and he would encourage.

THE TRADEMARK GLASSES

Fey became a sex symbol when she donned glasses and a little blue suit to be the anchorwoman on "Weekend Update." She tested twice for that position, once with contacts, which she bought just for that, and the second time with glasses, which she said made her feel protected. David Hiltbrand wrote, "Maybe it's the naughty-librarian fantasy, but guys were looking beyond Fey's glasses and severe business attire at the 'Update' desk and seeing a babe."* *Rolling Stone* hailed her as "the thinking-man's sex symbol."**

Eric Spitznagel asked her what that meant and she replied, "Glasses would make anyone look smarter. You put glasses on Woody Harrelson in *Indecent Proposal* and he's an architect. You put a pair of glasses on Denise Richards and she's a paleontologist."*** He then asked her if her career would come crashing down if she took off the glasses. She replied, "Definitely. I'm not that famous with the glasses, but I'm *really* not famous without them."****

"WEEKEND UPDATE"

As part of her act, Fey put on black-rimmed glasses and donned a blue blazer. It was a stroke of genius. Fey had become, according to Jason Gay of the *New York Observer*, the "embodiment of the sexy, smart girl—you know, a real New York type. . . . This effect is amplified not only by Ms. Fey's hormonally charged zingers . . . but also by her thick . . . glasses, which give her a mysteriously comely look that may be described as Winona Ryder meets Velma from Scooby-Doo."[19] Fey thought it was a lucky decision: "When I started on *Saturday Night Live*, I had the choice of

Fey admits that she does not need the glasses when she is in conversation. They are a stage prop and are mainly for show; in fact, the pair she wore on "Weekend Update" is owned by *Saturday Night Live*. Yet, when she tried going on air without them, she heard about it from fans on the Internet. Now, the glasses have followed her to *30 Rock*, because she plays a character like herself when she was at *Saturday Night Live*. But she predicts that her *30 Rock* character, Liz Lemon, would be taking the glasses off more frequently in the future.

* David Hiltbrand, "A 'Grounded' Tina Fey Expands Her Territory to Movies," *Philadelphia Inquirer*, April 28, 2004.

** Ibid.

*** Eric Spitznagel, "Tina Fey," *The Believer*, November 2003.

**** Ibid.

Tina Fey and Jimmy Fallon's tenure as the fake anchors on *Saturday Night Live*'s long-running "Weekend Update" skit was hailed by fans and critics alike. Fey and Fallon were paired together from 2000 to 2004.

wearing contact lenses, which I had never worn before, or glasses, in order to be able to read the cue cards."[20] She initially thought she would switch back and forth but decided to keep the glasses, which became her signature look.

Fey and Fallon gave "Update" a different spin, which increased the popularity of the show segment. Tom Shales and James Miller wrote in their book, *Live from New York*, "It's no longer a parody of a newscast; now it's just a sexy pair of smart alecks sitting around and making fun of the world."[21] Fey and Fallon were indeed a wonderful match. Michaels compared them to famed dancers Fred Astaire and Ginger Rogers. He said, "You were happy to see both. . . . The rhythm and timing of that is just a chemistry thing: either it works or it doesn't. . . . We saw the beginnings of that working."[22]

Fey's already busy schedule doubled, as she perused as many newspapers as she could to find material. Soon *SNL* was attracting more viewers than *The Tonight Show with Jay Leno* and *Late Show with David Letterman*. In 2001, *Saturday Night Live* won a Writers Guild Award for its twenty-fifth anniversary special. In 2002, the show won an Emmy for outstanding writing, which had not happened since 1989. Critics were heaping praise on Tina Fey's writing.

Two Tina Feys were emerging, at least to the public: the tiny, birdlike woman in sweats who spoke in a small, soft voice, and the larger-than-life woman appearing on the covers of magazines. In 2002, Alex Witchel wrote in the *New York Times*, "Comedians have traditionally been a noisy bunch. But Fey, 31, off camera at least, has an unexpected lack of bravado. She is shy, skinny, and seemingly unsure of herself."[23] To the public, she had morphed into a star, but to those close to her she was still the shy girl who had learned to put her crackling wit out there rather than make jokes behind her hands.

Michaels maintained that a performer had to be on a television show three years before he or she was easily recognized by the public. By 2004, she was becoming famous, and though her family had always believed in her, they were stunned by her sudden fame. Her brother, Peter, said in 2004 that their father wrote an e-mail, saying, "Here's all the magazines Tina is in this month. I can't take much more of all this."[24]

FEY'S STYLE OF COMEDY

Fey's humor can be "mean and disarming at the same time,"[25] wrote Virginia Heffernan in the *New Yorker*. Rachel Dratch described Fey's comedic style as "subtle yet purposeful: She will insist on writing a sketch that has an underlying point or payoff, as opposed to just riffing on a single joke or character."[26] She is a disciplinarian, according to Dratch, and all business. "It's not like we're giggling, wearing those arrows on our heads while we are writing. . . . There's not a lot of room for hanging out and pillow fights and stuff."[27] Amy Poehler said, "I love writing with Tina, but I'm always so self-conscious. Tina likes to be at the top of the mountain, keeping an eye on things." [28]

Fay's approach to sketch writing and acting was the opposite of slapstick. (When young her parents thought Carol Burnett too loud.) Fey did not make faces or exaggerate her responses, but instead became known as a listener who would take her time before responding. She was considered intelligent, and detached from the buffoonery of the guys.

PERSONAL HIGHS AND LOWS

Fey's early years on *SNL* were a time of great change in her life. On March 4, 1999, Del Close, the man who had created a style of improvisation that would forever associate his name with the art, died at age 64. In February 2001, Fey's teacher Martin de Maat died of AIDS. Fey, along with Jeff Richmond, Rachel Dratch, and Kevin Dorff, went to Chicago to visit de Maat in his hospital room. That same year, Jeff Richmond moved to New York from Chicago to become a part of *Saturday Night Live*. He had proposed to Fey when they were on vacation on Lake Michigan. Later, he said, "If I'd known so many people would ask me how I proposed, I would have done it in some more theatrical way."[29] Jeff Rogers, who knew Richmond at Second City, said of him, "He is supremely talented, and very, very nice. He's a happy person."[30] Tina Fey and he were married in a Greek Orthodox ceremony on June 3, 2001, in Upper Darby.

Months later, the terrorist attacks of September 11, 2001, which killed almost 3,000 people in New York City, at the Pentagon, and in Pennsylvania, greatly affected her. When being interviewed by Virginia Heffernan of the *New*

Yorker in 2003, Fey started to cry. "In New York you get to have little moments of fear every day now," she said. "Right after September 11th, I thought, We got to get out of here. My dad talked to me about how important it was to go back to work. But it has not been easy."[31] Soon after 9/11, anthrax, mailed to NBC news anchorman Tom Brokaw, was found in the NBC building where she worked. "You do get the irrational feeling that they are specifically coming for you,"[32] Fey said. When she heard about the anthrax scare, she put her coat on and went for a walk. Hours later Michaels called her and said that she was the only one who had not returned to the *SNL* set. It was her first display of fragility in front of her coworkers.

But she returned to work and found success in another realm of accomplishment—film. The movie she wrote, *Mean Girls*, with Michaels as executive producer, opened to positive reviews in 2004. The next year, a baby girl, Alice Zenobia Richmond, was born to Fey and her husband on September 10, 2005.

MOVING ON

In 2005, *Saturday Night Live* was criticized for switching to parodies of tabloid celebrities like Britney Spears or Lindsay Lohan rather than the more inventive and edgy parodies the show had been known for. Adam McKay, who had been head writer from 1996 to 1999, said, "We always knew that the No. 1 reason the show exists is to do impersonations of the president, our leaders, the Donald Trumps of the world—the people who need to be made fun of. And the show works when you do that, and it doesn't work when you don't do that."[33] On the other hand, Michaels pointed out that the core group of viewers for *SNL* was as it had always been: high school students. In response to the criticism of the shift in tone, Fey explained that everyone was thinking about job security and that writers drew from the celebrity tabloids scattered around their offices. "They're like pornography," she joked. "That's how disgusting you feel."[34]

The day came when Fey felt it was time to leave the show that she had been with for nine years. She had made a strong impact on *SNL*, and whether she liked to hear it or not, she was credited with creating better roles for women; furthermore, she had brought friends Amy Poehler and Rachel Dratch with her as she made her way to the top. (In fact, Poehler stepped up to take Fey's place on "Weekend Update.") Her imprint on the show would be said to be as strong as that of her one-time idol, Gilda Radner.

Fey had a television pilot in the works, *The Tina Fey Project*, which would soon get a name change to *30 Rock*. Michaels, who had strongly encouraged Fey to create *30 Rock*, would become an executive director of that show. (He had changed since the late 1980s when NBC president Fred Silverman had wanted to give Gilda Radner her own show. When she said no, Silverman had blamed Michaels.)

When asked if it had been difficult to leave *SNL*, Fey replied, "It was a risk. But it was an appropriate time for me to leave *SNL*. I felt like a senior who needed to graduate. I loved the show, but I also wanted to do a prime-time half hour. If it doesn't work, I'll go home and see my kid. It's a win-win situation."[35]

Women in Comedy

Although many professions have long been predominantly associated with men, women have made great strides in recent decades to achieve greater equality. Comedy has been no different, according to *New York Times* writer Sara Corbett. In an article she wrote about actress Anna Faris, "The Ditz Ghetto," she stated:

> Perhaps it began with Chevy Chase, or maybe Bill Murray, or even as late as Jim Carrey, but somewhere along the way, comedy became a showcase for outsize male personalities. And with it, the humor became bawdier, the acting became showier and the women started taking up less space.[1]

Writer and film director Nora Ephron said, "There is no question that there are a million more funny women than there used to be. But everything has more women."[2] She had an answer as to why there were more female comedians: "Here's the answer to any question: cable," she said. "There are so many hours to fill, and they ran out of men, so then there were women."[3] That is a crisp way of summing up a topic that refuses to die.

In a *New York Times* article, Amy Poehler was referred to as "an influential figure in the mostly masculine world of improvised comedy."[4] David Itzkoff wrote:

> She [Poehler] would prefer not to be reminded so frequently that she happens to be a woman surrounded by men. "You have to be grateful for it, and you want it to go away at the same time," she said. . . . "If you try to analyze comedy at all, it's deadly. If you try to bring your gender into it, it's unbearable."[5]

THE PING-PONG EFFECT

If Fey ever felt at a disadvantage in the world of comedy because of her gender, she has rarely been quoted making a negative remark, unlike some of her peers. Up until the early 1990s, both Bernie Sahlins and Del Close told women at Second City that they were not funny. Cast member Kevin Crowley said that Bernie Sahlins saw women as "the wife and girlfriend in scenes."[6] John Belushi did not like women writing his sketches because he believed they were unfunny. Jane Morris, a Second City veteran who left in 1989 to move to Los Angeles, was deeply aware that the traditional ratio of five men to two women put women at a disadvantage. Morris said that Close started to change his mind about women when he taught Tina Fey and Amy Poehler. After she left Second City, Fey said, "I had always felt that if a company is generating its own material, it was always preposterous to have this notion of 'Well, if we have too many women, there won't be enough parts.'"[7]

In 2000, when legendary comedian Jerry Lewis declared that he did not think women were funny, Fey had already made it to head writer at *Saturday Night Live* and was anchorwoman for "Weekend Update." The media was taking note. In an article titled "A Happy-Go-Lucky Nerd," Fey was credited

> with bringing some major girl power back to the show. When she joined *SNL*, she was one of only three women on the 22-member writing staff. As a result, one of the complaints was that female *SNL* players were not featured as regularly as the male performers. Fey changed all that. She created sketches that featured women and made it a point to showcase some of her old friends from Second City who had joined the cast, including Rachel Dratch and Amy Poehler.[8]

Alessandra Stanley pointed out in an article for *Vanity Fair* that much changed when Lorne Michaels, who had "presided over decades of male-dominated sketch comedy," named Fey head writer. "Suddenly," said Stanley, "*SNL* sketches were written by women, for women."[10]

Writer Virginia Heffernan stated that Fey's sketches tended to focus on gender. One "dramatized the barbarism of bikini waxing, and another cast Barbie as a fading beauty living with a gay man in Southern California—and she has spoofed stereotypes of women while taking on formerly neglected subjects, such as infertility, sexual abuse, and plastic surgery."[11] When asked if some of her sketches were anti-woman, Fey said that "the show's business was to make fun of people, and if it didn't make fun of women the female performers would have no parts to play."[12]

Fey has been publicly resistant to the stress that the media place on gender differences in comedy. She expressed impatience in 2004 when she said, "All the women that I work with say, 'When will things be better for women in comedy?' The first thing will be when we stop talking about women in comedy,"[13] she said. "This isn't track and field. There's no need to break it down by gender."[14] Yet, in 2007, Amy Poehler was one of only three female performers on *SNL* in a cast of 11, and there were still only three female writers on a staff of more than 20.

In a *Playboy* interview with Eric Spitznagel, Fey explained why an imbalance in the ratio of men to women writing comedy can skewer the jokes: "If mostly guys are writing the show, then the material will skew toward jokes that guys like. It's not malicious or intentional. It's what makes them laugh, so that's what they write."[15]

"Featuring women in her skits," Lorne Michaels noted, "is part of Fey's commitment to making sure they're 'well represented on air.'" As interviewer Spitznagel noted, "That's something new on a male-centric show generally not heralded for its stellar treatment of female comedians."[16]

Fey also told Spitznagel that she does find it unfair "when one woman tries to do comedy and isn't funny and it somehow reflects on all women. Nobody watches a terrible male standup comic and says, 'God, men just cannot do this.' There are just as many awful comedians who are men."[17] In another interview she was adamant that she did not think gender played into the challenges she had as head writer at *Saturday Night Live*, which makes it seem that gender issues in comedy are like verbal ping-pong—yes, no, yes, no.

In January 2007, Christopher Hitchens caused a stir when he wrote a *Vanity Fair* article in which he argued that women are not funny, and certainly not as funny as men.[18] The piece was an intellectual argument that delved into the differences in men and women, focusing on how they have

A publicity shot of Tina Fey from *Saturday Night Live*, circa 2002. After she lost a lot of weight, much was made in the press about her physical transformation.

evolved differently. Later in the article he issued the bold statement that *pretty* women could not be funny: "Most [female comedians] . . . are hefty, [lesbians], or Jewish."[19] Fey quipped in an interview with A.J. Jacobs of *Esquire*, "I've been all three of those,"[20] clarifying that she could "pass" for Jewish, though she is half Greek.

In an interview with Kelly West, Fey was asked what she would say if she ran into Christopher Hitchens in a bar. Fey joked, "I'd probably say you need to get out of this bar. You've been here for two days."[21] Then she grew more serious: "I didn't even read the article . . . the discussion is just so old and unnecessary anymore to be talking about

DECIDING TO BE PRETTY

Tina Fey told interviewer Maureen Dowd that seeing herself on the *Saturday Night Live* monitor as an extra was a shock: "I was like, 'Ooogh.' I was starting to look unhealthy. I looked like a behemoth, a little bit. It was probably a bad sweater or something. Maybe cutting from Gwyneth Paltrow to me." She added that she wanted "to be PBS pretty—pretty for a smart writer."*

Oprah Winfrey, in a 2008 interview, asked, "Speaking of being on the air, you weren't offered the 'Weekend Update' spot [at *SNL*] until after you lost 30 pounds." Fey answered:

> Well, I'd been writing, which is a sedentary life. And in Chicago, there's a different aesthetic than there is here in New York. . . . When I came to *SNL*, I was increasingly just sitting around eating bad food, but I wanted to get control of my weight. So I did Weight Watchers. And after I lost weight . . . Lorne [Michaels] . . . asked if I would test for "Weekend Update." But I don't want to make it sound as if he wouldn't have asked me to test if I hadn't slimmed down. No one ever said, "Lose the weight."**

For a while, it seemed that the public was obsessed with her weight loss. For some, like British comedienne Lisa Faith Phillips, Fey's weight loss brought up the men/women looks battle. She wrote:

whether women are funny. It just seems silly and outdated to me."[22]

Lisa Leingang is a "booker, promoter, talent scout and development executive"[23] who has worked with Fey, Carell,

But as we've read Tina Fey lost 30 pounds in hopes of being on air and people still advised Lorne Michaels from putting her on camera for she was not pretty enough. Most television shows are controlled by men. Bright less pretty comediennes don't tend to get invited on TV, though there are comediennes . . . who do hysterical comedy. The men doing comedy on TV just have to be funny while the women on *SNL* have to be funny and beautiful.***

Lauren Beckham Falcone of the *Boston Herald* wrote: "Et tu, Tina Fey? Here we thought you were the type of girl who would reassure us that being skinny wasn't important . . . [It] makes me wonder: Is diet success the new happily ever after?"****

---

* Dowd, Maureen, "What Tina Wants," *Vanity Fair*, January 2009, p. 121.
** Oprah Winfrey, "Oprah Talks to Tina Fey," *O, The Oprah Magazine*, February 2009.
*** Dr. Faith on the Road of Life, "Comedy Interview with Lisa Faith Phillips," December 27, 2008. http://www.dr-faith.com/blog.
**** Falcone, Lauren Beckham, "Comedy Heavyweight Fey Shed Pounds, Gained Success," *Boston Herald*, December 4, 2008.

Colbert, and many other comedians. In an interview with Melena Ryzik for the *New York Times*, she was asked why there are so few women in comedy. She replied, "I book Bumbershoot, the music festival in Seattle. . . . It's sold out all the time. This past year I was like, I have to have some women in there, and it was not easy to think of that."[24] She thinks that too many female comics "feel the need to, instead of being themselves, play the female card in their act, and then they are thought of as a female comedy version of a regular performer. When you cast yourself into that role, it goes into the stereotype category, and then it becomes like, we've seen that before."[25]

ANOTHER CONTROVERSY: PRETTY VS. NOT PRETTY WOMEN

Pretty women in comedy have often gone out of their way to mask their beauty. Perhaps the most famous example is Lucille Ball, the star of *I Love Lucy*, who had been a model when she started out in show business before transforming herself into a loud, goofy, and hysterical 1950s housewife. Once it was established that women are funny, the next question was: Can pretty women be funny? Before that was argued sufficiently enough for some, a new trend developed, possibly started by Tina Fey, after she transformed into a sexy and hilarious woman. Jay Leno said:

> They used to say in the '60s and '70s that if you were an attractive woman, you couldn't be a comedian because it would be really distracting. Well, I think Chelsea Handler and Sarah Silverman have proved that wrong. Now you have a generation of women that doesn't have to do self-put-downs. They talk about exactly the same subjects as male comics—drinking, carousing, dating.[26]

A "Weekend Update" skit from the November 11, 2000, episode of *Saturday Night Live* featuring Will Ferrell as Janet Reno, Darrell Hammond as Bill Clinton, and Tina Fey and Jimmy Fallon as the skit's anchors.

Amy Poehler was quoted in the book *Live from New York*, "I'm of the school that loves crazy makeup and wigs and teeth. I always want my characters to look uglier than I'm allowed or than I have time for. . . . I think it's pretty hard to be sexy and funny at the same time. Some people can do it, but few can pull it off."[27] That was in 2002. Today, on her own show, *Parks and Recreation*, she is praised for being both sexy and funny.

Men have not often had their physical appearances determine their comedic talents. Will Ferrell, Adam Sandler, Mike Myers, or Seth Rogen, to name a few modern male comics, have rarely had their looks debated. Kathy Griffin said, "I'm constantly dieting, constantly working out, because unlike Will Ferrell, I'm going to take more hits if I don't at least have a normal figure. I was walking through Central Park yesterday without any makeup, and I come home and I'm on . . . TMZ for being old and ugly."[28]

Alessandra Stanley wrote:

> It used to be that women were not funny. Then they couldn't be funny if they were pretty. Now a female comedian has to be pretty—even sexy—to get a laugh. At least, that's one way to view the trajectory from Phyllis Diller and Carol Burnett to Tina Fey. . . . The funniest women on television are youthful, good-looking, and even, in a few cases, close to beautiful.[29]

She added, "It has become a supply-and-demand issue: the supply of good-looking female comedians is growing, and the industry demands that they keep growing prettier."[30] Fey explained, "With television, it's just expected that every person be better-looking. In the 90s, it seemed like every person on a sitcom—think of the cast of *Friends*—was just really foxy. I know our show and *The Office* have normal people. If anything, it's shifted back."[31]

When asked about auditions he is holding for the next generation of female comedians, Lorne Michaels said, "Two or three are really funny. And they are totally confident and don't feel any need to do ugly-girl comedy. They do skits like 'Angelina Jolie on an airplane.'"[32] He may have been referring to Abby Elliott, whose father, Chris Elliott, was called "the funniest man on television"[33] by none other than David Letterman. Twenty-two-year-old Abby became the youngest female cast member ever on *Saturday Night Live* in 2008. (Chris Elliott worked as a writer and performer on *SNL* during the 1994–1995 season, making him and Abby the show's first parent-child cast members.)

Fran Lebowitz noted, "It's not that these girls are better than the girls who preceded them. They're luckier. They came along at a time when the boys allowed them to do this. In comedy, timing is everything."[34]

Change does not come easily, however. On the National Public Radio blog site, "Monkey See," a headline read, "*SNL*'s Michaela Watkins 'Just Too Classically Pretty to be Hilarious'?" After Lorne Michaels had announced that two new women were to have the status of featured players on the show, Tom Shales of the *Washington Post* wrote, "Not as replacements for anybody, Michaels says, although cute Casey Wilson and glamorous Michaela Watkins have concurrently left. Watkins may have been just too classically pretty to be hilarious."[35] Watkins has no idea why she was fired, but she has not criticized Michaels in interviews.

WOMEN WRITING

In April 2008, Alessandra Stanley decided to write a retort to the Christopher Hitchens article about women in comedy. According to Stanley, "behind the curtain the writers' room

IN HER OWN WORDS

In her acceptance speech at the New York Women in Film and Television event in 2005, Tina Fey recalled how her mother was told by her Greek father she would not be going to college because "that was for boys." Fey said:

> I hope that my mother derives satisfaction from the fact that her daughter has found some success [in professions] that were just for boys.*

*"Tina Fey Makes Broadsheet's Day," Salon.com. http://www.salon.com/life/broadsheet/2005/12/13/tina_fey.

has remained a male-dominated clubhouse. 'The girl in the room,' the lone woman writer on a white, male staff, is a long-standing and long-suffering tradition in comedy."[36]

Although this remains true on many television shows as well as in film, Fey caught on years ago that women would succeed through their writing. She said, "Women drive what's on television, and husbands and boyfriends decide on movies. I'm doing it backwards: I have a TV show for men [*30 Rock*] and a movie [*Baby Mama*] coming out for women."[37] With that film, she also changed the dynamic that is common in most so-called "chick flicks," where there is a beauty and her best friend (a revisit of the pretty-not-pretty syndrome). Poehler and Fey were presented as equals in the film.

Up and coming comediennes took note that if they wanted to succeed they had better start writing their own material. The "Write Club," founded in Los Angeles by Paula Killan in 2006, is an example of a new method of teaching comedy through writing. Her writers bring a strong intelligence to their material. It is no exaggeration to say that the writing movement has begun to re-define women in comedy.

Men and women obviously come at comedy from different perspectives. Fey commented on the difference: "Every comic way of writing is unique, but I think male comedy is more boisterous. Usually it involves robots and sharks and bears. Female comedy is more likely to be about the minutiae of human behavior and relationships."[38]

Stanley wrote, "As comedy has opened up, women who once might not have dared write comedy, or writers who hadn't considered performing, have been emboldened to become writers and get onstage."[39] Perhaps it is Tina Fey's seamless transitions from writer to actress and back again that has given her a leg up on the competition.

Creator
of *30 Rock*

The sitcom created by Tina Fey, *30 Rock*, takes its name from the famous location where *Saturday Night Live* is filmed: 30 Rockefeller Center in Midtown Manhattan. Premiering on October 11, 2006, the sitcom was set up as a show within a show and was based on—what else?—*Saturday Night Live*. On the show, Liz Lemon (Tina Fey) is the supervising writer and Jack Donaghy (Alec Baldwin) is the sexist corporate producer, based loosely on *Saturday Night Live* executive producer Lorne Michaels (who also happens to be the executive producer on *30 Rock*). With so much quick-flying verbal humor, viewers sometimes complain that they miss many jokes.

When Eric Spitznagel asked Fey if she had wanted to star on *30 Rock*, she replied that her original intention had been to be solely the writer, but then she reconsidered. She ran the idea by Amy Poehler first, expressing her concern that she was too old and maybe people had grown tired of her. Poehler, she said, "helped me think like a male comedian."[1] She said, "When Ray Romano and Jerry Seinfeld got their shows, I don't think they had a moment like, Am I good enough to do this? I need to stop worrying so much about what other people think."[2]

The Donaghy character barked a brilliant synopsis of the Liz Lemon character at her in an early episode: "Sure, I got you. New York third-wave feminist. College-educated. Single and pretending to be happy. Overscheduled, undersexed. You buy any magazine that says 'healthy body image' on the cover, but your kitchen's got nothing but SnackWells and expired yogurts."[3]

Fey and Michaels knew they had stiff competition from another NBC pilot that was under way and very similar to *30 Rock*, called *Studio 60 on the Sunset Strip*, which was more drama than comedy. Initially all bets were on *Studio 60*, created by *The West Wing* producer Aaron Sorkin, a formidable name in the business. *30 Rock* was on shaky ground the first year, but typically, Fey worked around the clock to iron out the kinks.

Katherine Pope, the head of Universal Media Studio who was responsible for making *30 Rock*, recalled:

> At a network, you're not supposed to get emotionally involved in the shows. . . . I'm not like that. It's no secret that the *30 Rock* pilot tested terribly, and there was a point where it was possible it wasn't going to get picked up. I just felt like the hysterical girl in the room, going, "Are we seriously talking about not picking up *30 Rock*? Wait a minute! We have Tina Fey, and we have Alec Baldwin! What are we even talking about here?"[4]

Not only was *30 Rock* not canceled (and *Studio 60* was), but it started winning a lot of critical acclaim. Much of the success of the show was attributed to the writing. Critics called the show "sarcastic and smart, its acting snappy and sharp."[5]

PERFECT CASTING

Fey wrote the part of Jack Donaghy with Alec Baldwin in mind, although she did not know him, because he seemed the ideal actor to play the boss. It was Michaels and fellow producer Marcia Klein who took the script to him. When Baldwin said yes, Fey was thrilled. She also wrote a part for Jack McBrayer, who plays Kenneth the Page at NBC, and for Scott Adsit, who had both been at Second City in Chicago. (When Fey played a hooker in the Second City revue, "Citizen Gates," she used to give lap dances to Adsit eight times a week.)

Fey was perhaps happiest about once again including her old friend Rachel Dratch, and she said that one of the most enjoyable aspects of the pilot was that she and Dratch were to be reunited. But before it aired, Dratch was replaced by Jane Krakowski, who was a better "opposite" for Liz Lemon. It took time for Fey to develop Krakowski's acting chops, partly because she wrote her part at the last minute.

THE NEW SITCOM STRUCTURE

Just as Fey changed the face of *SNL* by writing and creating more subjects for women, she created a different style of sitcom. For *30 Rock* she typically had three stories going at the same time, and often placed the characters into flashback scenes. As they were thinking about something, they would suddenly be back in that moment. Ross Simonini, writing for the *New York Times*, explains that sitcoms like *Scrubs* and *30 Rock* "explore their situations through collage

Tina Fey with her *30 Rock* costar Alec Baldwin. Fey wanted to get Baldwin for the part of her boss on the series but did not think the actor would be interested. She was thrilled when he agreed to do it and now considers it perfect casting.

and a restless stream of consciousness."[6] They are a form of sketch comedy. It started, he said, with *The Simpsons*, a show in which animation made it easy for flashbacks and dream sequences to happen. The "digressions," or the dream and flashback scenes, according to Simonini, "give the characters meaning and the show its substance."[7] Fey brought her husband, Jeff Richmond, with her to the new show to compose the music.

She explained in an interview with Kelly West that television shows *30 Rock*, *Scrubs*, and *The Office* (two shows that Fey admires) are single camera shows, whereas shows like *Friends* and *Seinfeld* were multi-camera. Single camera shows are like little movies, she explained, and do not have live audiences. Fey mentioned that she would like to shoot a show in front of an audience, and that they had tried at one time. She said, "I grew up on that multi-camera format [Mary Tyler Moore, Carol Burnett, and others]. I think that's a great format and as soon as somebody—you know, someone will—there'll be a new one that works and all of a sudden everybody will make those again."[8]

In its first season, *30 Rock* attracted an average of 5.4 million viewers, not an impressive number. But it steadily grew in popularity. In November 2008, David Bauder noted that 8.7 million people saw the premiere of *30 Rock*, according to Nielsen Media Research, making it the fortieth most-watched primetime show. This was an 18 percent increase in viewers from the 2007 premiere. It was noted that *30 Rock* was up against the incredibly popular *Dancing with the Stars* on ABC, which had 18.88 million viewers. Of the top 10 shows, however, all were at least double the number of viewers at *30 Rock*.

CRITICISM AND CRITICAL ACCLAIM

Critics, for the most part, loved it. *New Yorker* television critic Nancy Franklin, writing in December 2008, believed that Fey did what Jerry Seinfeld used to do, which was to make room for his fellow performers. She felt that "Fey's intelligence comes across, of course, but it's a kind of managerial intelligence, a high level of competence . . . sort of no-nonsense—or very-little-nonsense—approach."[9]

Fey admitted that it was hard adjusting to acting on camera in a scripted series. She simply did not feel worthy, but eventually gave herself a pep talk and "just decided that within my own performance I'm going to stop apologizing that I'm here."[10] Fey's acting ability came up again in an interview with Kelly West, who mentioned that it seemed that she was becoming more comfortable as an actress. Fey answered:

I think you might be right that I've really fully stopped apologizing for being in the show. And I am having a very good time shooting these episodes now. . . . I feel so grateful to have been recognized for the stuff that I did on the show last year, that maybe that has helped me relax a little bit.[11]

On October 15, 2009, Alessandra Stanley, writing for the *New York Times*, was critical of Fey's acting ability, noting:

The striking thing about the new season, especially when seen in the same Thursday night lineup as *Parks and Recreation* [which stars Amy Poehler], is the acting limitations of its star and creator, Tina Fey. Ms. Fey is one of the funniest comedy writers on television and a gifted mimic (Sarah Palin), and she is at her worst playing a comic version of herself.[12]

She continued, "Liz [Lemon's] foibles—she dresses badly, is a junk-food glutton, can't get a date—are the kind of flaws that thin, beautiful actresses affect because they think it makes them more approachable."[13] In an ironic twist, Fey had become too beautiful to play a parody of her old self. One episode that Stanley particularly liked, however, was when Liz Lemon went back to a high school reunion and realized she had been unpopular, not because she was a nerd, but because she was a mean girl who tortured her classmates with "a withering wit and cool disdain."[14]

Stanley compared the two friends, Fey and Amy Poehler, declaring Amy Poehler the better comedian and Fey the distinguished writer. Acting has been secondary to Fey's writing all along, yet the feeling is there that the yearning to achieve as an actress has not dimmed. Alec Baldwin, in a satirical interview, asked Fey why she did not write herself in, and she replied, "I like being a writer who performs." He replied, "It seems to me that you like being a performer who hides behind writing."[15]

After receiving an Emmy in 2008 for lead comedy actor, Baldwin said:

> We [at *30 Rock*] have the greatest writers, but the show was created by one woman. This was Tina's idea. This was Tina's thing. She is the head writer. She is there every day, even when she's not shooting as an actress. She goes back and forth between acting and writing. We're very, very lucky.[16]

Hitting the Stratosphere

As the new television season was starting in September 2008, both *Saturday Night Live* and *30 Rock* were in need of a ratings boost. Though the latter show won a record number of awards that year, the ratings remained worrisome. *SNL's* popularity had waxed and waned over the years, and it just so happened that it was then in a lull.

On August 29, Senator John McCain, who was running against Senator Barack Obama for president, selected the Alaskan governor, Sarah Palin, as his running mate on the Republican ticket. Kelefa Sanneh, in the *New Yorker*, described the governor as "a Tina Fey character come to life."[1] Even Fey's three-year-old daughter, Alice, thought Sarah Palin was her mother when she first saw her on television.

Fey was resistant at first when Lorne Michaels called her and asked her to think about impersonating the governor on *Saturday Night Live*. Fey replied, "I'll do a joke about her. I'll do a sketch where I'm myself. I'll do anything *except* impersonate her!"[2] She had had no experience doing impersonations and worried about falling flat. Michaels persisted, and she finally agreed after Amy Poehler agreed to impersonate two other women, Hillary Clinton, then a presidential candidate, and Katie Couric, the CBS anchorwoman who had conducted a live interview with Palin. Fey said, "I also felt safe doing it with Amy. I wouldn't have enjoyed doing it alone, because I never did anything alone on *SNL*."[3]

THE MYSTERY WOMAN CANDIDATE

When Governor Palin was announced as McCain's running mate, few had heard of her. A former mayor, former beauty queen, and the mother of five children, including an infant son who was born with Down syndrome, Palin had a star quality about her that caught the attention of the national media.

Despite her lack of national exposure, Palin had ambition that was never in question. Prior to being announced as the candidate for the vice presidency, she had invited a group of conservative journalists and politicians to Alaska. She won over most of them. Historian Victor Davis Hanson said that she was "striking. She has that aura that [Bill] Clinton, [Ronald] Reagan, and Jack Kennedy had—magnetism that comes through much more strongly when you're in the same room."[4] By the time they left they knew that she wanted to drill for oil in Alaska's protected wilderness, that she was a hunter, and that she was pro-life on the abortion issue.

After McCain announced her as his pick for running mate, voters wanted to know Palin's qualifications. Looks

During the 2008 presidential election, Tina Fey *(left)* was lauded for her impersonation of Governor Sarah Palin of Alaska, the running mate of Republican nominee Senator John McCain of Arizona. Fey appears here with Amy Poehler, who impersonated Senator Hillary Clinton of New York.

and charisma mattered in the contemporary world of politics, but she needed more than that to secure votes. As the number of debates and interviews increased, questions were raised about her knowledge and experience. She used an "us against them" platform, claiming that she was a political outsider and not involved in Washington politics, which was an advantage. She tended to speak in run-on sentences, and when she did not know an answer, she would often change the subject. During debates she had a way of winking as she answered questions and smiling broadly.

Journalist Michael Gerson called her "a mix between Annie Oakley and Joan of Arc."[5] Then, something happened that would change both her life and Tina Fey's: Fey impersonated Sarah Palin on *SNL*.

FEY AS PALIN

Over the years, *SNL* had offered up numerous impersonations of politicians, some successful and others not. Audiences had more recently become accustomed to seeing Will Ferrell playing George W. Bush, introducing him as a "cheerful idiot who had been thrown into the deep end; he captured the winsome earnestness of a guy doing the best he can."[6] It was no secret that much of the *SNL* staff was politically liberal, though they made fun of Republicans and Democrats alike. Fey, though she leaned toward the more liberal Democrats, had been brought up in a Republican household and remained deeply respectful of her parents' political views.

Fey, impersonating Sarah Palin, and Amy Poehler, impersonating Senator Hillary Clinton, stood at a podium in the opening sketch on *Saturday Night Live* on September 13, 2008. Millions of viewers were tuned in, both live and online. Fey had decided to make everything about Sarah Palin bigger, which is a key to creating humor around a public figure. Physically, it required a "team of wig makers, colorists and a pound of human hair."[7] Jim Dwyer wrote in the *New York Times*, "Reproducing the Palin hairdo required the creation of a wig that combined a 'French twist with a '60s bouffant kind of thing, and bangs,'"[8] quoting Bettie Rogers, head of the hairstyling department at *SNL*. They also taped her ears down because Fey thought they stuck out too much, and the makeup department changed the shape of her lips.

According to the *New Yorker* writer Kelefa Sanneh, Fey "just turns up the glee and the swagger, the provincialism and the Alaska accent. If Palin is going to make Vice-Presidential-debate history by winking—how many times? five?—at the camera, then Fey is going to wink even more, and shoot off an imaginary gun, too."[9]

Another popular send-up of the governor was based on an interview Palin had given to journalist Katie Couric on September 24, 2008. The way Fey delivered Palin's lines was side-splittingly funny. She seemed completely over-the-top and earnest, and yet she used actual dialogue from the Couric/Palin interview, one that Palin, who had been wary of interviews, later regretted.[10]

The sketch caused a huge stir. Mark A. Perigard, in the *Boston Herald*, wrote that "nothing has affected Fey's public profile as much as John McCain's decision to make the Alaska governor his running mate. One can argue that if *30 Rock* can't pick up new viewers now, it never will."[11] Fey's impersonation also helped *SNL*, which had its highest ratings in six years. Soon enough, people began to ask if Sarah Palin would make an appearance on *SNL* and confront Tina Fey.

Did she ever! In a bold and smart move, Palin agreed to appear on *SNL* on October 18, 2008. The show started with the fake Palin (Fey) coming onstage, followed by Alec Baldwin mistaking the real Sarah Palin for Fey backstage. He said to producer Michaels, "This is the most important election in our nation's history and you want her, our Tina, to go out there and stand with that horrible woman?"[12] When Baldwin was told about his "mistake," he apologized to the real Palin by saying that she was "way hotter in person."[13] Palin said in response, "I must say, your brother Stephen is my favorite Baldwin brother,"[14] after which she walked onstage to replace Fey. The two women were matched in red jacket and shirt. Fey glided away so Palin could announce *SNL*'s opening line, "Live from New York, it's Saturday Night!"

That night 17 million people were watching. On May 18, 2009, Brian Steinberg of *Advertising Age* wrote that according to Visible Measures, the five skits Fey did as Sarah Palin generated 27.7 million views on NBC.com alone. Across 150 video-sharing sites like YouTube and MySpace, 68.5 million viewers also tuned in. Viewership for *30 Rock* also increased, much to Fey's happiness.

TRUTH VS. FICTION IN MEDIA

Did it matter that Sarah Palin did not actually say that she could see Russia "from her house"? (What she had actually said was that one can see Russia from Alaska.[15]) No. According to James Poniewozik of *Time*, "When voters close their eyes now and envision Public Palin, likely as not they see Tina Fey. It's impossible to say whether *SNL* drove the drop in Palin's public approval or simply followed it."[16] He added, "But in an era glutted with satire—*The Colbert Report*, the *Onion*, JibJab—there is still a special power in an old-fashioned *SNL* impersonation. It's shamanistic; it's like owning a voodoo doll: capture your target's soul, and you can make her dance just by waving your arms."[17]

IMPACT ON THE PRESIDENTIAL ELECTION

Oprah Winfrey asked Fey if she thought her impersonation—much of which was based on things Palin actually said—had had a big impact on the outcome of the presidential campaign, which Barack Obama and his running mate, Senator Joe Biden, won. (Some have compared Fey's send-up of Palin to Chevy Chase's bumbling impersonation of President Gerald Ford on *SNL*, which many believe cost Ford the election in 1976.) Fey responded, "When humor works, it works because it's clarifying what people already feel. It has to come from someplace real. You don't just decide to destroy a person by making up stuff, and no one at *SNL* is writing to go after someone."[18] It also helped,

Fey said on David Letterman's show, that Palin "has a really crazy voice."[19] When Letterman asked her to describe it, she replied, "Alaskan windsong?"[20] Letterman asked the

FAKE NEWS SHOWS

In recent years, many young people have gotten their news from fake news programs like "Weekend Update" on *Saturday Night Live*. In fact, Comedy Central has a full line-up of such fake news shows, including *The Daily Show* with Jon Stewart, *The Colbert Report*, and *Chocolate News*. HBO had *Real Time with Bill Maher*. Fox News premiered *The ½ Hour News Hour* in an attempt to create a conservative counterpart to *The Daily Show*. CNN stepped in with *D.L. Hughley Breaks the News*. Joshua Alston of *Newsweek* wrote, "Never before has our comedy and our news commingled to this degree. . . . Satire solidifies opinions we already have because we've internalized the logic that all humor finds its root in truth. If *SNL* says Hillary [Clinton] was being unfairly picked on in the primary debates, then it is so."*

In a background paper prepared by Aralynn McMane, director of the Youth Readership Development, World Association of Newspapers, and released at a meeting in Paris, France, in February 2007, it was reported that many young people are "news grazers," who get their information from a variety of sources, not just the mass media. It continued: "Research in 2005 on 5,000 Internet users between 13 and 24 years old from 11 countries found a very strong emphasis on the importance of self-expression, along with the need to feel connected with one another while retaining a strong self-direction."** Their own messages to each other counted most, inevitable question about her power to sway the election, and Fey replied, "I can't even get people to watch *30 Rock*! I can't persuade my kid to use the potty."[21] On the other

not mass media. Americans spend two-thirds of their day interacting with media, and one-third of that time consuming multiple media simultaneously.

When Tina Fey was asked if she thought it was wrong that kids were getting their news from shows like *SNL* and *The Daily Show*, she replied:

> I don't think so. I did the same thing when I was younger. I never sat down and watched the evening news. I'd get all my current events from Letterman or *SNL*. You can get some good information that way. If you watch *The Daily Show* all the time, you'll have a basic understanding of what's happening in the world. Besides, I think a lot of young people don't just watch comedy shows to stay informed. They also want to be guided on how they're supposed to feel.***

* Alston, Joshua. "Why Obama Needs a Tina Fey," *Newsweek*, October 25, 2008. http://www.newsweek.com/id/165813/output.

** McMane, Aralynn. World Association of Newspapers. Sponsored by the World Press Freedom Committee, co-sponsored by UNESCO. February 15 & 16, 2007, Paris, France.

*** Spitznagel, Eric. "Tina Fey," *The Believer*, November 2003. http://www.believermag.com/issues/200311/?read=interview_fey.

hand, Marlene Naanes wrote, "The skits have been replayed on TV news shows, signaling to many that *Saturday Night Live*'s political influence has penetrated further than ever in its history."[22] John Leo, a senior fellow at the Manhattan Institute, said:

> I think [Fey's impression of Palin is] a tremendous help to the Democrats. It doesn't create a feeling about Palin. But I think it solidifies or magnifies what's in people's minds. It's probably fairer to say people who were leaning or already going to vote democratic just solidified their vote.[23]

ACCUSATIONS AND DEFENSES

In January 2009, conservative radio talk show host John Ziegler was promoting a video of Palin called "Media Malpractice: How Obama Got Elected and Palin was Targeted." He felt Palin was assassinated by the media. At one point in the video, Palin watched Tina Fey saying, "I believe marriage is meant to be a sacred institution between two unwilling teenagers"[24]—a reference to the fact that Palin's unmarried teenage daughter Bristol and her boyfriend, Levi Johnston, announced they were expecting a baby, which had left Palin vulnerable to more ridicule and criticism. Palin took a number of media outlets to task, including *People*, the Associated Press, and the *Anchorage Daily News*, about the rumors they printed about her family. And as for Fey's satirical remark about the "two unwilling teenagers," Palin said, "Cool, fine, come attack me, but when you make a suggestion like that that attacks a kid, that kills me."[25]

Fey defended herself: "I never did feel that we were mean to her. We stuck to a lot of things that she herself had said, and I think there is a very strange double standard because it's a woman portraying another woman."[26]

FEY'S REACTION TO NEW CELEBRITY

Though Fey had been a lead actor on *30 Rock* for two years and had performed on *Saturday Night Live*'s "Weekend Update" for six years, she generally went unnoticed as she went back and forth between the Upper West Side of Manhattan—where she and her husband, Jeff Richmond, own an apartment—and Rockefeller Center, where her office is. The Sarah Palin impersonation changed that dynamic. In her interview with Oprah Winfrey, Fey discussed her new celebrity: "Weird and vulnerable, especially since it's linked to politics. I don't want some crazy person trying to get to me."[27] She added later in the interview that the new level of fame that came from the Palin impersonation made her anxious: "I don't love it that people recognize me all the time."[28]

Although Palin has resigned as governor of Alaska, she has written a book, *Going Rogue*, and attracts thousands of fans wherever she makes public appearances. As of this writing, she is being mentioned as a possible candidate for the Republican ticket in the 2012 presidential election. Nor has she forgotten Fey's cutting impersonation. She drew a huge laugh at the Gridiron Club in Washington, D.C., for journalists, when she said, "I came down from my hotel room and I could see the Russian Embassy."[29]

Films
and Books

Because Fey wanted to write a film, she began seeking material. She saw an article in the *New York Times* on Rosalind Wiseman, who had written a scholarly work, *Queen Bees and Wannabes: Helping Your Daughter Survive Cliques, Gossip, Boyfriends, and Other Realities of Adolescence.* Wiseman allowed Fey to see the book in advance, and Fey sat down and read about the various roles of teens; in this case, the Queen Bee is the leader, then there is the Sidekick, the Banker (a girl who uses secrets to move up in the group), and the Target (the person who is singled out for harassment). Fey's reading of Wiseman's work would inspire her to write the biting 2004 comedy *Mean Girls*.

Lorne Michaels had started a film company called Broadway Video. (Paramount produces most of his films with *SNL* cast members.) When Fey approached him with the idea for a screenplay, he was interested in producing it. She wrote herself in a supporting role as a math teacher, wrote Amy Poehler in as the mother of the "Queen Bee," and wrote a part (principal of the high school) for Tim Meadows, who had been at Second City and on *Saturday Night Live* with her. For Fey it was a way for her to act, and in this case, she could be on set all the time once filming began.

Lindsay Lohan played the lead, Cady Heron, a nice girl who had spent most of her life in Africa and knew nothing about the ways of American teens until her family moves into a wealthy area of Chicago. The "Queen Bee" is named Regina George. The other popular girls in the film were called "The Plastics" and are portrayed as tyrants.

TRUTH IN FICTION

Fey claimed that she was a mean girl in high school, due to a jealous streak. She told Virginia Heffernan of the *New Yorker*: "Girls are capable of spending a lot of time with someone and hating them."[1] She recalled the various cliques at her high school in Upper Darby in the 1980s. She recalled she was part of the "AP-class brainiac nerds," who sat around making up nasty names for their classmates. "The metalheads with stringy hair were the 'Hammers,' because they broke the ice at parties, usually with some crazy stunt like a belly flop over the coffee table. The popular, preppy girls were the 'Laura Ashley Parade.'"[2]

In a 2002 interview, Fey referred to herself as "banker," meaning if there was "gossip to be heard about anyone, I wanted to know it in detail."[3] She explained, "I think I was playing offense a little bit. Like to a guy friend, I'd say, 'Really? That's who you like?' I would try to control people through shame. I only learned how to stop doing that like two years ago."[4] She was downright scornful of the "kids

Tina Fey mined her high school experiences to write the script for the 2004 comedy *Mean Girls*. She is seen here with the film's star, Lindsay Lohan.

who drank, cut school, overdressed, or slept around."[5] Today, she calls it a defense mechanism.

If Fey needed any reminders of those years in high school, Lohan, 17, getting into a public feud over a boy with fellow teen actress Hilary Duff, 16, while filming *Mean Girls*, took her back. Fey was compassionate. "Sometimes I think *US Weekly* should leave them alone," she said. "They're just kids. If notes I wrote about some girl in ninth grade were in *US Weekly*, I'd be really bummed. Actually, I'd be really psyched."[6]

In an interview with Oprah Winfrey, Fey was asked if she wanted to apologize to anyone from high school. Fey replied:

[W]hen I wrote *Mean Girls*, I had some archetypes in my head—like the prettiest girl and the most popular girl. And as I was working on the script, I threw in some names of real people from high school and mixed them up with other random names. I later heard from a friend who went to my high school reunion that some of my former classmates weren't pleased. When they saw the movie, they were like, "What did I do to her?" I was inadvertently hurtful. So I apologize to the women whose names I used.[7]

A NEW LEARNING CURVE

Writing for movies, Fey learned, was an entirely different process from writing sketches for *Saturday Night Live*. In devising comedy sketches, she said, "story is your enemy. Story will sink you. Conversely, in a movie, if you don't have [a] story, then that will sink you. So I was just trying to learn that."[8] And adapting a book was also somewhat difficult:

> It was kind of a bonehead thing to do on my part for my first screenplay—to try to adapt a nonfiction, non-narrative book. I had to make up the whole story. I mean, it's not "Chinatown." But just to keep a story moving forward was all new to me . . . I did a million drafts. And I did the thing everybody does. I read Syd Field [*Screenplay*] and I used my index cards.[9]

The response from teens was interesting. Fey said, "We did a bunch of test screenings, and the 13- and 14-year-old girls would sit wide-eyed and sort of horrified. They were into it as a drama, but it was too close to the bone for them to laugh at. It's only women who are a little bit older who can laugh at it."[10] *Mean Girls* was praised for its intelligent writing, and it ended up grossing more than $86 million. Fey could be proud of her first film effort.

ALICE ZENOBIA RICHMOND

Fey would say that her greatest creation is her daughter, Alice. Fey's costar on *30 Rock*, Alec Baldwin, said of Alice in April 2009, "[Fey's] daughter Alice looks like a Hummel figurine: she is so beautiful, she doesn't look real."[11] Fey claims that Alice is funnier than she is.

AMERICAN EXPRESS

In 2007 and 2008, Fey appeared in two commercials for American Express, in which, once again, she appeared as herself: the harried, put-upon head writer who is in charge of almost everyone on the imaginary show. "I'm so excited to be a part of the American Express 'Are you a Cardmember?' campaign,"[12] said Fey.

> It's pretty impressive when you look at all of the people who have been featured in American Express campaigns before me. Ellen DeGeneres, Robert De Niro, Martin Scorsese; quite frankly I'm not sure why they asked me, but I have to say, I think this is more exciting than playing on the US Open . . . for me, cause I would totally lose.[13]

IN HER OWN WORDS

After a 43-day maternity leave from NBC following the birth of her daughter, Tina Fey returned to work:

> I had to get back to work. NBC has me under contract, the baby and I only have a verbal agreement.

Tina Fey and her daughter, Alice, are photographed on a New York City street. Although she maintains a busy schedule, Fey always makes time for her daughter.

The American Express vice president of global advertising, Diego Scotti, explained why she was chosen: "Tina's witty sense of humor is truly one-of-a-kind and has such great appeal. We had a great time creating this commercial because so many people can relate to the chaos and ups-and-downs that Tina's story tells about a day in her life."[14] The corporate-speak sounds similar to sketch comedy. And, who, we might ask, could possibly relate to a day in the life of Tina Fey?

MAKING MOVIES

In 2008, Fey and Amy Poehler costarred in *Baby Mama*, in which Fey portrays a stressed-out career woman who hires a surrogate to have her baby. The surrogate mother is Amy Poehler, who plays a trashy woman. This was a big-screen comedy in the vein of other *SNL* alumnae who had "made it" in movies, though it did not come close to earning what the blockbuster movies of her male peers had grossed. Reviewers were mixed. *New York Times* reviewer Manohla Dargis thought that Poehler was "at least 10 years too old for the role,"[15] but at the same time she was the "ball that bounces against Ms. Fey's formidable wall."[16] She continued: "Not that anyone need worry about this female odd couple, given that Ms. Fey, who doesn't have the acting chops that might invest her character with some personality, has been forced to play it straight and narrow."[17] She did think her genuinely funny, but thought "the studio boss might have ordered up a dance coach for Ms. Fey, maybe a few lessons on how to walk across a set or move her upper body once in a while."[18]

On the other hand, Michael Rechtshaffen wrote, "Fey makes an effective transition from her Emmy-winning *30 Rock* character to that of Kate, the unmarried vice president of Round Earth Organic Market."[19] He also thought director Michael McCullers was obviously inexperienced but, he said, "The end result still should play very respectably with its targeted female audience—especially those who can identify with Fey's ticking clock—but it will likely fall short of Judd Apatow levels."[20]

In 2009, Fey had a small part in *The Invention of Lying*, a film created by Ricky Gervais of the TV sitcom *The Office*. It is about a world where no one has ever told a lie. Gervais plays the character who tells the first lie, and the rest of the film revolves around the consequences resulting from that one lie. Fey is Gervais's brutally honest secretary who makes fun of him. The film received moderate praise.

DID YOU KNOW?

Sophia Banay, writing for Portfolio.com, said that they estimate Fey has earned, "at the very least, $17 million so far, with tens of millions—if not hundreds of millions—more possible down the road." Two films she made, *Mean Girls* and *Baby Mama*, are believed by an analyst with Exhibitor Relations in Los Angeles to have brought her between $8 million and $10 million. Her deal with American Express is estimated to be $1 million. The assumption is that NBC is offering her at least as much as she earned on *Saturday Night Live* for her work on *30 Rock*—$1.5 million annually in 2005. If *30 Rock* is syndicated, she could earn much higher numbers. For example, Larry David, co-creator of *Seinfeld*, is believed to have made $200 million when that show went into syndication. Another Web site, www.mahalo.com, listed Tina Fey's earnings for 2008 at $4.6 million. For Tina Fey, it pays to be in comedy!

A WELL-ROUNDED WOMAN

Fey continues to find success in a number of fields. In October 2008, Little, Brown and Company in Boston had offered Fey a reported $5 million advance for writing a book of humorous essays. Editor Reagan Arthur said that it would be published in 2011. In April 2010, she had her first lead role in a film since *Baby Mama* with *Date Night*. In the film, she is coupled with Steve Carell, one of the stars of the American television version of *The Office*. A couple finds that their routine date night goes awry when they lie that they have reservations at a restaurant and realize too late they have taken the table that belongs to criminals.

But Fey's main focus is her work on *30 Rock*. In the 2009–2010 season, it seems that Fey has taken critics' advice and given herself more time in front of the camera. In a scene on the December 3, 2009, show, she had a great comedy moment when she allowed the fame that might accompany Liz Lemon's new show go to her head, and she let loose in a blonde wig and broke into song and dance. It was a hint of what the young Tina in *Cabaret* must have been like when she was a senior at the University of Virginia and performing the role of Sally Bowles.

Legacy

Noting the growing presence of comedy in pop culture, Jeremy High wrote on September 11, 2009: "Faces that may otherwise be relegated solely to comedy clubs and sitcom bit-parts are now taking top billing in sitcoms, movies, commercials, and are even responsible for delivering a large portion of young America's daily news."[1]

Of the phenomenon of popular female comics, Caitlin Moran wrote in the London *Times*:

> While men may still be capable of being funny—and, indeed, continue to be quite good at it—the ground rules of comedy are in flux. And one of the biggest ground rules has just been abolished entirely. For this year it became possible, for the first time in

history, to make the following statement: currently, the two funniest people in the world are women. . . . Tina Fey and Sarah Silverman are where comedy is at right now.[2]

UNCANNY TIMING

From the time Fey embarked on a career in theater and improvisation, she seemed to be living out her destiny. Her timing has been uncanny. Second City had often been criticized for being a white male club that had not equally attracted nor promoted women or minorities. Fey proved to be the exception to the rule, in part because of changes taking place in Second City. New directors like Mick Napier were just being allowed in as she landed at Mainstage. He included her in the cast of "Citizen Gates" on the recommendation of Scott Allman, who had directed her in the touring company and was quite enthusiastic about her. Napier had never seen her perform, so he looked at a tape of her in the touring company and thought she was okay. He said that 80 percent of his decision to put her in his show was based on Allman's recommendation. She excelled.

Saturday Night Live also happened to be on the cusp of change the year Fey arrived to write sketch comedy in 1997. By 2003, executive producer Lorne Michaels spoke about the changing climate of the show: "This cast is young," he said. "They're ambitious. They pride themselves on being less self-destructive. But we didn't pride ourselves on being self-destructive in the seventies. People were experimenting with freedom. Comedy people are always outsiders."[3] He also denied that Fey was a square, an image that she liked to convey. He compared her calling herself a square to "the tendency of the show's first cast to claim they were rebels."[4] Fey is one of the most hip women operating in comedy.

She started out at the controls at *30 Rock*, and her imprint is on every aspect of it. Again, the timing was uncanny. She maintains that if it had been up against a popular show like *Grey's Anatomy*, *30 Rock* would not have had a chance. But competition was low in 2006, when her show debuted. She signed on as producer, writer, and performer, and it was her determination for the show to succeed that brought it back for a second season. Though based on the chaotic and male-dominated show *Saturday Night Live*, *30 Rock* is reminiscent of one of Fey's favorite shows when she was a girl, *The Mary Tyler Moore Show*. At the same time, it is cutting-edge comedy, with its bedrock in sketch comedy.

Ironically, the decision that she made to impersonate Sarah Palin on *Saturday Night Live* is probably the one that made her a household name. She was pressured, and she finally agreed to do it. It was those appearances that introduced her to the world that was unfamiliar with *30 Rock*.

ROLE MODEL

When asked by an interviewer in 2008 if she thought she was a role model for young girls, or if she felt qualified, she said, "Sure, why not?" She added:

> I could probably be a better-educated feminist. For my generation, we're all figuring it out as we go along. You have to follow your gut. The line in the sand between what's okay and what's not keeps changing. You can have a strong, empowered character—like a Carrie Bradshaw on *Sex and the City*, a show mostly for ladies—and sometimes she's in her underpants. It's easy to forget you can be both.[5]

It was reported in the *Arts & Sciences Magazine* at the University of Virginia in July 2004 that an unusually large number of alumni were heading to Chicago to try

Tina Fey attends the Sixteenth Annual Screen Actors Guild Awards ceremony at the Shrine Auditorium in Los Angeles in 2009.

out improvisation. The majority of them were not theater majors like Fey, but, over the four years they were under- graduates, had become members of the Whethermen, a UVA collective of improvisation performers formed in 1997. Most headed first to the IO Improv Training Program in Chicago, where Fey, whom many claim to be their inspiration, started.

She is known to have an extraordinary work ethic, and one gets the sense that embedded deep inside is the philoso- phy that instead of complaining about a situation, the best bet is to jump in and work harder than anyone else. She has put in the hours, and even today she works on scripts in the car as she is driven to the studio. When girls wait outside the NBC building in Manhattan, hoping to meet her, she tells them to focus on writing, not acting. She thinks there are too many actors out there.

CONTRASTING SIDES

Fey is a study in opposites. Eric Spitznagel wrote:

> Tina is two very different women trapped in the same body, the yin and yang of comedy. Half her personality is what you would expect: She's intel- ligent and poised, like a feminist superhero. But the other half is an introverted underdog who makes up for her lack of confidence with a biting sense of humor. If life really does imitate high school, then she's the hot cheerleader everybody wants to sleep with and the band geek who makes fun of you for being so shallow.[6]

It seems that when she is not on camera or on the cover of a magazine, she has a way of disappearing into herself. Adjectives used to describe her are tiny, shy, and birdlike, with a voice so quiet that it is sometimes difficult to understand her. Friend Amy Poehler said, "She's pretty monastic at times."[7] At the same time she exudes authority on the *30 Rock* set where everyone but Lorne Michaels defers to her, and even he cares about what she thinks. At the end of an article in the *New Yorker*, for example, he asked, "What does she say about me?"[8]

Her former professor, Richard Warner, explained that "kids recognize that Tina is the true definition of a clown, and the clown is the observer of life."[9] Some years ago, she returned to the University of Virginia to participate in an improvisation study. Warner said, "She's great. She came back around nine years ago, when Second City did a residency. She's very much the same in the way she relates to people. She arrived here with a level head, and she kept that. There is a core of decency and generosity she carries with her today."[10]

REFUSING TO TAKE CREDIT

Fey, uncomfortable with praise, is the first to give credit to others. She will quickly disagree if she feels all the focus is on her. That said, in recent years no one has been credited more with putting women in comedy in the forefront, yet her weapons against discrimination have been subtle: She writes women into revues and scripts and infuses her shows with a female sensibility. When she donned army attire and marched into professor Richard Warner's office at the University of Virginia because he had selected an all-male war play to direct, that action spoke volumes about who she was then, and who she is today.

A TIGHTLY CONTROLLED ENVIRONMENT

Actress Gwyneth Paltrow, who has guest starred on *Saturday Night Live*, said:

> Fame is such a weird and distorting thing. I've thought a lot about it, and my theory is that you

kind of stop growing at the age you are when you become famous. Because what happens is, people start removing all your obstacles, and if you have no obstacles you don't know who you are. . . . When you're in the public eye, people project things onto you, and if you take them on yourself, they're very scattering and they can alienate you. Being famous can be very damaging in lots of ways.[11]

Fame has seemingly left Fey undamaged, yet it has changed her relationships with her coworkers. For example, Fey's husband, Jeff Richmond, who composes the music for *30 Rock* as well as being an executive producer, said that once he had to tell her that one of the episodes

DID YOU KNOW?

In 2009, Tina won a Mothers Who Make a Difference award from the organization Love Our Children USA. The national organization lists statistics on its Web site: More than 3 million children have been victimized and neglected; 1.8 million are reported missing; more than 580,000 are in foster care; one out of seven is approached by online predators; and 41 percent have been bullied online.

Other organizations that she supports are Autism Speaks and Global Envision. She acted as spokeswoman for the 2009 Light the Night Walk for the Leukemia & Lymphoma Society. An online charity site, CharityFolks.com, raising money for the organizations such as The Urban Ecology Institute, offered bidders a walk-on role in Fey and Steve Carell's film, *Date Night*. They raised $14,000. Fey was also the host of the welcome video at the Mercy Corps Action Center to End World Hunger in New York, which opened in Battery Park on October 16, 2008.

While Tina Fey is very comfortable with the fact that she might be considered a role model for aspiring comedians, she is also comfortable with the idea that success in life cannot be measured by fame alone.

had failed, as there was no one else who would, expect perhaps Michaels.

Understandably, Fey keeps the public at bay when it comes to her personal life. Her father; her best friend from high school, Marlene Kimble; and her friend from high school who worked with her in theater, Damian Holbrook, refuse interviews unless they have her specific permission. In her professional life, she is cocooned in a tightly knit group of ex–Second City and *Saturday Night Live* alumni. Looking at the roster of producers for *30 Rock*, familiar names jump out: Lorne Michaels, Jeff Richmond, and Paula Pell (who was a senior writer for *SNL*), for example, are executive producers. Michael McCullers, who directed *Baby Mama*, shared an office with Fey at *Saturday Night Live*. Costar Amy Poehler is her best friend, and she and Rachel Dratch remain friends. *Baby Mama* was produced by Michaels, and Richmond created the music. Her film *Date Night* feels somewhat like a step out of the cocoon, as it is not her creation, but it is not a giant step, as she and Steve Carell performed together at Second City.

The Sixtieth Second City reunion was held the weekend of December 12 and 13, 2009, and to the surprise of many, Fey did not attend. Stephen Colbert, Jeff Garlin, Jack McBrayer, and Scott Adsit were all there, but missing in action were Amy Poehler, Bill Murray, Mike Myers, and Dan Aykroyd. Comedian Bill Needle could not resist sending a satirical stab in the direction of the missing "stars" when he said, "They couldn't get over the moats around their castles."[12]

THE FUTURE

Oprah Winfrey said to Fey, "You've been given the talent of great humor. How do you want to continue using it as the best expression of who you are?"[13] Fey replied, "I want to keep creating comedy that is, as my old improv teacher [Martin de Maat] would say, at the top of our intelligence or higher. It's easy to fall into the trap of just cranking out things that are good enough to sell."[14] Winfrey asked next, "What do you know for sure?"[15] Fey's answer?

> I know for sure that you can tell how smart people are by what they laugh at. I know for sure that a hard-boiled egg is two points on Weight Watchers. I know for sure that my kid needs my husband and me to be with her more. And I know for sure that I can't get comfortable with all the attention I've been getting because it won't last forever. It's just a moment—and there will be other moments when people don't care what I'm doing.[16]

That may be the most self-effacing statement she has ever made. Meredith Blake, writing for the *Los Angeles Times*, speculated that the December 3, 2009, episode of *30 Rock* was the most autobiographical. In it, Liz Lemon's boss thinks the new show to be hosted by Lemon called *Dealbreakers* is going to be a huge hit, but he cannot seem to stop picking on her, subtly criticizing her hair and the glasses, until she, having lost all confidence, locks herself in an office and refuses to come out. Blake wrote:

> I think this episode shed some insight into what it's like to be Tina Fey—not just a writer who's made the leap to performing, but one who's also a woman. Virtually every profile ever written about Fey discusses both her physical and professional transformation, from chubby writer with a bad haircut to a svelte, thinking man's sex symbol and television star with the ability to single-handedly derail a presidential campaign. Despite this, you get the sense some

of the time—well most of it, really—that Fey still isn't convinced of her allure. It's hard to tell whether she believes it or if it's just a shtick, but my sense is that it's a little bit of both.[17]

A discussion Fey had with writer Eric Spitznagel backs up what Blake said. Her prediction in her high school yearbook was that she would one day become "very, very fat." That image still resonates for her. When Spitznagel, conducting an interview for *Playboy*, asked her if she would be relieved when her career ends, she answered, "It will be a sad day. Because the minute the camera stops and it's not pointed at me anymore, I will probably gain a hundred pounds."[18] He reminded her of her yearbook quote and she said, "That's right. I still say it all the time, so when it happens, I'm covered."[19]

CHRONOLOGY

1970   Fey is born in Upper Darby, Pennsylvania, on May 18.

1992   She graduates from the University of Virginia.

1993   Fey performs at ImprovOlympic (IO) in Chicago.

1994   She is invited to join the cast of The Second City in Chicago.

1997   She becomes a writer for *Saturday Night Live*.

1999   She performs in a show called *Dratch & Fey*.

2000   She becomes the first female head writer at *Saturday Night Live*.

2001   Fey becomes co-anchor of *Saturday Night Live*'s "Weekend Update" with Jimmy Fallon; she wins a Writers Guild of America award; Fey marries Jeff Richmond on June 3.

2004   Her film *Mean Girls* opens; she leaves *Saturday Night Live*.

2005   Fey's daughter, Alice Zenobia Richmond, is born on September 10; she is given a Muse Award by New York Women in Film & Television.

2006   Her show *30 Rock* airs, to critical acclaim.

2007   She receives Emmy Awards for Outstanding Lead Actress in a Comedy Series, Outstanding Writing for a Comedy Series, and Outstanding Comedy Series.

2008   She wins Emmys for Outstanding Writing for a Comedy Series, Outstanding Lead Actress, and Outstanding Individual Performance; her film *Baby Mama* opens; Fey impersonates vice presidential candidate Sarah Palin; she is listed among *Time*'s Most Influential People in the World and is named Entertainer of the Year by the Associated Press.

2009   Fey wins an Emmy for her impersonation of Sarah Palin.

2010   Her film *Date Night*, costarring Steve Carell, opens.

NOTES

CHAPTER 1

1. Nancy Franklin, "Sketchy Comedy: Tina Fey's *30 Rock*," *New Yorker*, December 8, 2008, http://www.newyorker. com/arts/critics/television/2008/12/08/081208crte_ television_franklin.
2. Interview, *The View*, October 15, 2009.
3. Maureen Dowd, "What Tina Wants," *Vanity Fair*, January 2009, http://www.vanityfair.com/ magazine/2009/01/tina_fey200901.
4. Eric Spitznagel, "Playboy Interview: Tina Fey," *Playboy*, January 2008, http://www.playboy.com/articles/tina-fey-interview/.
5. Franklin, "Sketchy Comedy: Tina Fey's *30 Rock*."
6. Ross Simonini, "The Sitcom Digresses," *New York Times*, November 21, 2008, http://www.nytimes. com/2008/11/23/magazine/23wwln-comedy-t.html.
7. Ibid.

CHAPTER 2

1. David Hiltbrand, "A 'Grounded' Tina Fey Expands Her Territory to Movies," *Philadelphia Inquirer*, April 28, 2004.
2. Jancee Dunn, "Tina Fey: Funny Girl," *Reader's Digest*, April 2008, http://www.rd.com/your-america-inspiring-people-and-stories/tina-fey-interview/ article 54446.html.
3. Ibid.
4. Jennifer Senior, "*Saturday Night Live*'s Tina Fey," *Daily Breeze*, April 30, 2004.
5. "Tina Fey Gets the Last Laugh," *New York Post*, April 25, 2004, http://www.foxnews.com/ story/0,2933,118079,00.html.
6. Dowd, "What Tina Wants."

7. *Session Magazine*, "Tina Fey American Writer," December 5, 2008, http://www.sessionmagazine.com/tina-fey-american-writer.
8. Dunn, "Tina Fey: Funny Girl."
9. Spitznagel, "Playboy Interview: Tina Fey."
10. Lynda Gorov, "With New Comedy, Fey Gets 'Mean,'" *Boston Globe*, April 25, 2004.
11. Spitznagel, "Playboy Interview: Tina Fey."
12. Ibid.
13. Dunn, "Tina Fey: Funny Girl."
14. Jennifer Senior, "The New Queen of Mean," *New York Times*, April 25, 2004, http://www.nytimes.com/2004/04/25/movies/25SENI.html.
15. "Tina Fey: Actress Comedian Saturday Night Live," http://www.famuscelebrities.org/tv_stars/tina_fey.html.
16. Spitznagel, "Playboy Interview: Tina Fey."
17. Ibid.
18. Dunn, "Tina Fey: Funny Girl."
19. Author interview with Harry Dietzler, December 9, 2009.
20. Ibid.
21. Ibid.
22. Hiltbrand, "A 'Grounded' Tina Fey Expands Her Territory to Movies."
23. Author interview with Professor Douglas Grissom, October 13, 2009.
24. Ibid.
25. Ibid.
26. Ibid.
27. Ibid.
28. Ibid.
29. Ibid.
30. Ibid.
31. Ibid.

32. Author interview with Professor Richard Warner, University of Virginia, October 18, 2009.

33. Ibid.

34. Ibid.

35. Ibid.

36. Ibid.

37. Ibid.

38. Ibid.

39. Ibid.

40. Ibid.

CHAPTER 3

1. Charna Halpern et al, *Truth in Comedy: The Manual of Improvisation*, Colorado Springs, Colo.: Meriwether Publishing Ltd., 2001, p. 13.

2. Author interview with Jane Morris, November 17, 2009.

3. Sheldon Patinkin, *The Second City: Backstage at the World's Greatest Comedy Theater*, Naperville, Ill.: Sourcebooks, Inc., 2000, p. ix.

4. Oprah Winfrey, "Oprah Talks to Tina Fey," *O, The Oprah Magazine*, January 2009, http://www.oprah.com/world/Oprah-Winfrey-Interviews-Tina-Fey.

5. ImprovOlympic, Interview with Jason Chin, http://users.rcn.com/improv/www.improvolymp.com/shows/improvst.

6. Ibid.

7. Mike Thomas, "Laugh Lessons: What Today's Top Comics Learned at Second City," *Chicago Sun-Times*, September 27, 2009, http://www.suntimes.com/entertainment/books/1790574,SHO-Sunday-unscripted27main.article.

8. Patinkin, *The Second City*, p. 144.

9. Interview, Jane Morris.

10. Ibid.

11. Ibid.

12. Ibid.

13. Charna Halpern et al, *Truth and Comedy*, p. 20.

14. Ibid.

15. Mike Thomas, *The Second City Unscripted: Revolution and Revelation at the World-Famous Comedy Theater*, New York: Random House, 2009, p. 191.

16. Ibid., p. 190.

17. Interview with Jeff Rogers, December 17, 2009.

18. Thomas, *The Second City Unscripted*, p. 163.

19. Spitznagel, "Playboy Interview: Tina Fey."

20. Darel Jevens, "Returning for an I-Opening Look Back: Stars Reminisce About Their Alma Mater on Its 25th—er, 24th—Anniversary," *Chicago Sun-Times*, August 21, 2005.

21. Maureen Ryan, "Tina Fey's Climb to the Top of the Comedy Heap," *Chicago Tribune*, September 30, 2007, http://archives.chicagotribune.com/2007/sep/30/entertainment/chi-0930_tinasep30.

22. Interview, Jane Morris.

23. Interview with Jeff Rogers, December 17, 2009.

24. Thomas, "Laugh Lessons."

25. Thomas, *The Second City Unscripted*, p. 222.

26. Interview with Jane Morris, November 17, 2009.

27. Thomas, *The Second City Unscripted*, p. 221.

28. Virginia Heffernan, "Anchor Woman: Tina Fey Rewrites Late-night Comedy," *New Yorker*, November 3, 2003.

29. Steve Johnson, "Colbert, Fey and Carell: Comedy's Power Players," *Chicago Tribune*, December 6, 2009.

30. Ibid.

31. Interview with Jeff Rogers, December 17, 2009.

32. Amy E. Seham, *Whose Improv Is It Anyway? Beyond Second City*, Jackson, Miss.: University Press of Mississippi, 2001, p. 127.

33. Interview, Jane Morris.

34. Thomas, *The Second City Unscripted*, pp. 221–222.

35. Darel Jevens, "They're Everywoman: Roles Multiply as Improv Gets More Female-friendly," *Chicago Sun-Times*, April 6, 1997.

36. Sun Publications (IL), "Latest Second City Revue 'Paradigm Lost' First Class," March 14, 1997.

37. Ibid.

38. Heffernan, "Anchor Woman: Tina Fey Rewrites Late-night Comedy."

39. Winfrey, "Oprah Talks to Tina Fey."

40. Ibid.

41. Dunn, "Tina Fey: Funny Girl."

42. Thomas, *The Second City Unscripted*, p. 237.

43. Ibid., pp. 239–240.

CHAPTER 4

1. Oprah.com, "Tina Fey's Aha! Moment," from the June 2003 issue of *O, The Oprah Magazine*.

2. Ibid.

3. Ibid.

4. Ibid.

5. Ibid.

6. Dave Itzkoff, "The All Too Ready for Prime Time Players," *New York Times*, January 2, 2005, http://www.nytimes.com/2005/01/02/arts/television/02dave.html.

7. Ibid.

8. Ibid.

9. Ibid.

10. Heffernan, "Anchor Woman: Tina Fey Rewrites Late-night Comedy."

11. Franklin, "Sketchy Comedy."

12. Tom Shales and James Andrew Miller, *Live from New York*. Boston: Little, Brown & Company, 2002, p. 529.

13. Ibid.

14. Winfrey, "Oprah Talks to Tina Fey."

15. Dowd, "What Tina Wants."

16. Ibid.

17. Ibid.

18. Shales and Miller, *Live from New York*, p. 465.

19. Jason Gay, "Meet Four-Eyed New Sex Symbol, 'Weekend Update' Anchor Tina Fey," *New York Observer*, March 4, 2001.

20. Caroline Ryder, "A Conversation with *30 Rock*'s Tina Fey," *Women's Health*, July 14, 2008, http://www.womenshealthmag.com/life/tina-fey-talks-to-womens-health.

21. Shales and Miller, *Live from New York*, p. 464.

22. Gay, "Meet Four-Eyed New Sex Symbol."

23. Alex Witchel, "Laughing When It Hurts: *Saturday Night Live* Anchor Tina Fey Struggles While Making Comedy Out of Tragedy," *New York Times*, January 21, 2002.

24. Hiltbrand, "A 'Grounded' Tina Fey Expands Her Territory to Movies."

25. Heffernan, "Anchor Woman: Tina Fey Rewrites Late-night Comedy."

26. Gay, "Meet Four-Eyed New Sex Symbol."

27. Ibid.

28. Heffernan, "Anchor Woman: Tina Fey Rewrites Late-night Comedy."

29. Kyle Smith, "Leap of Fey," *People*, May 3, 2004, http://www.people.com/people/archive/article/0,,20149986,00.html.

30. Interview, Jeff Rogers, December 17, 2009.

31. Heffernan, "Anchor Woman: Tina Fey Rewrites Late-night Comedy."

32. Ibid.

33. Itzkoff, "The All Too Ready for Prime Time Players."

34. Ibid.

35. Cindy Pearlman, "Fey: Even if *30 Rock* Fails, It's Still a Win-win Situation," *Chicago Sun-Times*, October 8, 2006.

CHAPTER 5

1. Sara Corbett, "Encounter: The Ditz Ghetto," *New York Times*, November 12, 2006, http://query.nytimes. com/gst/fullpage.html?res=9B02EFDB113FF931A257 52C1A9609C8B63&sec=&spon=&pagewanted=4.

2. Alessandra Stanley, "Who Says Women Aren't Funny?" *Vanity Fair*, April 2008, p. 184.

3. Ibid.

4. Dave Itzkoff, "Please Don't Tell Her She's Funny for a Girl," *New York Times*, March 18, 2007, http://www. nytimes.com/2007/03/18/arts/television/18dave.html.

5. Ibid.

6. Thomas, *The Second City Unscripted*, p. 165.

7. Thomas, "Laugh Lessons."

8. *Notable Biographies*, Tina Fey Biography, "A Happy-Go-Lucky Nerd," http://www.notable biographies. com/news/Ca-Ge/Fey-Tina.html.

9. Stanley, "Who Says Women Aren't Funny?" p. 190.

10. Ibid.

11. Heffernan, "Anchor Woman: Tina Fey Rewrites Late-night Comedy."

12. Ibid.

13. Gorov, "With New Comedy Fey Gets 'Mean.'"

14. Ibid.

15. Spitznagel, "Playboy Interview: Tina Fey."

16. Ibid.

17. Ibid.
18. Christopher Hitchens, "Why Women Aren't Funny," *Vanity Fair*, January 2007, http://www.vanityfair.com/culture/features/2007/01/hitchens200701.
19. Ibid.
20. A.J. Jacobs, "Tina Fey, Make Us Laugh," *Esquire*, May 1, 2008, http://www.esquire.com/women/tina-fey-0508?click=main_sr.
21. Kelly West, "Interview: Tina Fey Talks About *30 Rock*, (Part 2)," Cinemablend, April 1, 2008, http://www.cinemablend.com/television/Interview-Tina-Fey-Talks-About-30-Rock-Part-2-9724.html.
22. Ibid.
23. Melena Ryzik, "The Guide on the Laugh Track," *New York Times*, October 30, 2009, http://www.nytimes.com/2009/11/01/arts/television/01mele.html.
24. Ibid.
25. Ibid.
26. Yael Kohen, "We'll Show You Who's Funny," *Marie Claire*, April 1, 2009.
27. Shales and Miller, *Live from New York*, p. 529.
28. Kohen, "We'll Show You Who's Funny."
29. Stanley, "Who Says Women Aren't Funny?" p. 185.
30. Ibid.
31. Ibid.
32. Ibid., p. 190.
33. Ed Zuckerman, "A Professionally Funny Family," *New York Times Magazine*, November 24, 2009, p. 31.
34. Stanley, "Who Says Women Aren't Funny?" p. 190.
35. "Monkey See," "*SNL*'s Michaela Watkins 'Just Too Classically Pretty to be Hilarious'?" September 9, 2009, http://www.npr.org/blogs/monkeysee/2009/09/snls_michaela_watkins_just_too.html.

36. Stanley, "Who Says Women Aren't Funny?" p. 191.
37. Ibid., p. 190.
38. Dunn, "Tina Fey: Funny Girl."
39. Stanley, "Who Says Women Aren't Funny?" p. 190.

CHAPTER 6

1. Spitznagel, "Playboy Interview: Tina Fey."
2. Ibid.
3. Jacques Steinberg, "Tina Fey's Brash Bid for Prime Time," *New York Times*, April 6, 2006.
4. Andrew Goldman, "Interview with Katherine Pope," *Elle*, October 28, 2009.
5. Jacques Steinberg, "*30 Rock* Lives, and Tina Fey Laughs," *New York Times*, September 23, 2007, http://www.nytimes.com/200709/23/arts/television/23stei.html?.
6. Simonini, "The Sitcom Digresses."
7. Ibid.
8. West, "Interview: Tina Fey Talks About *30 Rock* (Part 2)."
9. Franklin, "Sketchy Comedy."
10. Steinberg, "30 Rock Lives, and Tina Fey Laughs."
11. Kelly West, "Interview: Tina Fey Talks about *30 Rock*, (Part 1)," Cinemablend, April 1, 2008, http://cinemablend.com/television/Interview-Tina-Fey-Talks-About-30-Rock-Part-1-9723.html.
12. Alessandra Stanley, "Still Biting the Hand that Feeds," *New York Times*, October 14, 2009, http://www.nytimes.com/2009/10/15/arts/television/15rock.html.
13. Ibid.
14. Ibid.
15. Alec Baldwin, "Tina Fey: First She Broke the Hold Male Writers Had Over *Saturday Night Live*. It was only a Matter of Time Before She Loosened the Grip that TV had on Her," *Interview*, April 1, 2004.

16. Huffington Post, "Tina Fey's Emmy Night: Humble, Wants to Stop Playing Sarah Palin," September 22, 2008, http://www.huffingtonpost.com/2008/09/22/tina-feys-emmy-night.

CHAPTER 7

1. Kelefa Sanneh, "Laughing Matters: Saturday Night Politics," *New Yorker*, October 27, 2008, http://www.newyorker.com/arts/critics/television/2008/10/27/081027crte_television_sanneh.
2. Winfrey, "Oprah Talks to Tina Fey."
3. Ibid.
4. Jane Mayer, "The Insiders: How John McCain Came to Pick Sarah Palin," *New Yorker*, October 27, 2008, http://www.newyorker.com/reporting/2008/10/27/081027fa_fact_mayer.
5. Ibid.
6. Sanneh, "Laughing Matters: Saturday Night Politics."
7. Jim Dwyer, "Getting in Palin's Hair, or Close to It," *New York Times*, September 16, 2008, http://www.nytimes.com/2008/09/17/nyregion/17about.html?.
8. Ibid.
9. Sanneh, "Laughing Matters: Saturday Night Politics."
10. Saturday Night Live, "Tina Fey Plays Palin in Katie Couric Interview Parody," *The Nation*, September 28, 2008, http://www.thenation.com/doc/20081013/fey_video.
11. Mark A. Perigard, "Lemon Aid: Tina Fey Hoping Palin Impersonation Will Boost *30 Rock*," *Boston Herald*, October 26, 2008.
12. Daily Mail (London), "As Palin Sees the Funny Side; The Real Deal: Sarah Palin, The Comic Fake: Tina Fey," *Daily Mail*, October 20, 2008.
13. Ibid.
14. Ibid.

15. James Poniewozik, "Palin vs. 'Palin': When *SNL* Parody Becomes Campaign Reality," *Time*, October 9, 2008, http://www.time.com/time/printout/0,8816,1848735,00.html.

16. Ibid.

17. Ibid.

18. Winfrey, "Oprah Talks to Tina Fey."

19. Guest Appearance, *Late Show with David Letterman*, October 17, 2008.

20. Ibid.

21. Ibid.

22. Marlene Naanes, "Tina Fey Shaping Sarah Palin's Image on *Saturday Night Live*," *amNewYork*, October 9, 2008.

23. Ibid.

24. Howard Kurtz, "Online, Sarah Palin Has Unkind Words for the Press," *Washington Post*, January 9, 2009.

25. Ibid.

26. PTI, The Press Trust of India, Ltd., "Fey Denies Being Mean to Sarah Palin on TV Show," December 2, 2008.

27. Winfrey, "Oprah Talks to Tina Fey."

28. Ibid.

29. Zimbio, "Sarah Palin Pokes Fun at Herself at Journalists' Dinner," December 6, 2009, http://www.zimbio.com/sarah+palin/articles/c9Ne4FHqpML.

CHAPTER 8

1. Heffernan, "Anchor Woman: Tina Fey Rewrites Late-night Comedy."

2. "Tina Fey Gets the Last Laugh."

3. Jennifer Senior, "Funny Girl: *Saturday Night Live*'s Tina Fey Finds Laughs in High School Cruelty," *Daily Breeze*, April 30, 2004.

4. Ibid.

5. Ibid.
6. Joel Stein, "Goddess of the Geeks," *Time*, April 26, 2004, http://www.time.com/time/magazine/article/0,9171,993922,00.html.
7. Winfrey, "Oprah Talks to Tina Fey."
8. APOnline, "Tina Fey Adjusts to Writing for Film," May 1, 2004.
9. Senior, "Funny Girl: *Saturday Night Live*'s Tina Fey Finds Laughs in High School Cruelty."
10. Ryder, "A Conversation with *30 Rock*'s Tina Fey."
11. Alec Baldwin, "The 2009 TIME 100," *Time*, April 30, 2009.
12. American Express Press Release, "Writer, Performer Tina Fey Joins American Express 'Are You a Cardmember?' Campaign," http://home3.americanexpress.com/corp/pc/2007/tfey_print.asp.
13. Ibid.
14. Ibid.
15. Manohla Dargis, "Learning on the Job about Birthing Babies," *New York Times*, April 25, 2008, http://www.nytimes.com/2008/04/25/movies/25baby.html.
16. Ibid.
17. Ibid.
18. Ibid.
19. Michael Rechtshaffen, "Bottom Line: Not Quite a Bouncing Bundle of Joy but Still Serves up Plenty of Kicky Comedy," *Hollywood Reporter*, April 21, 2008, http://www.hollywoodreporter.com/hr/film/reviews/article_display.jsp?rid=10987.
20. Ibid.

CHAPTER 9

1. Jeremy High, "America's Greatest Comedy Theater," http://www.rvanews.com.

2. Caitlin Moran, "Tina Fey and Sarah Silverman: The New Queens of Comedy," London *Times*, October 3, 2008, http://entertainment.timesonline.co.uk/tol/arts_and_entertainment/stage/comedy/article4869771.ece.

3. Heffernan, "Anchor Woman: Tina Fey Rewrites Late-night Comedy."

4. Ibid.

5. Spitznagel, "Playboy Interview: Tina Fey."

6. Ibid.

7. Heffernan, "Anchor Woman: Tina Fey Rewrites Late-night Comedy."

8. Ibid.

9. Author interview with Richard Warner, October 18, 2009.

10. Ibid.

11. Shales and Miller, *Live from New York*, p. 548.

12. "Second City Alums Remember Their Roots," *Chicago Sun-Times*, December 12, 2009.

13. Winfrey, "Oprah Talks to Tina Fey."

14. Ibid.

15. Ibid.

16. Ibid.

17. Meredith Blake, "*30 Rock*: Being Tina Fey," *Los Angeles Times*, December 4, 2009, http://latimesblogs.latimes.com/showtracker/2009/12/30-rock/html.

18. Spitznagel, "Playboy Interview: Tina Fey."

19. Ibid.

BIBLIOGRAPHY

BOOKS

Halpern, Charna et al. *Truth in Comedy: The Manual of Improvisation*. Colorado Springs, Colo.: Meriwether Publishing Ltd., 2001.

Patinkin, Sheldon. *The Second City: Backstage at the World's Greatest Comedy Theater*. Naperville, Ill.: Sourcebooks, Inc., 2000.

Sahlins, Bernard. *Days and Nights at the Second City*. Chicago: Ivan R. Dee, 2001.

Seham, Amy E. *Whose Improv Is It Anyway? Beyond Second City*. Jackson, Miss.: University Press of Mississippi, 2001.

Shales, Tom and James Andrew Miller. *Live from New York*. Boston: Little, Brown & Company, 2002.

Thomas, Mike. *The Second City Unscripted: Revolution and Revelation at the World-Famous Comedy Theater*. New York: Random House, 2009.

ARTICLES

Absolute Astronomy. "Tina Fey: Facts, Discussion Forum and Encyclopedia Article." Available online. URL: http://www.absoluteastronomy.com/topics/Tina_Fey.

American Express Press Release. "Writer, Performer Tina Fey Joins American Express 'Are You a Cardmember?' Campaign." Available online. URL: http://home3.americanexpress.com/corp/pc/2007/tfey_print.asp.

APOnline. "Tina Fey Adjusts to Writing for Film," May 1, 2004.

Baldwin, Alec. "Tina Fey: First She Broke the Hold Male Writers had over *Saturday Night Live*. It was only a Matter of Time Before she Loosened the Grip that TV had on Her." *Interview*, April 1, 2004.

Blake, Meredith. "*30 Rock*: Being Tina Fey." *Los Angeles Times*, December 4, 2009. Available online. URL: http://latimesblogs.latimes.com/showtracker/2009/12/30-rock/html.

Corbett, Sara. "Encounter: The Ditz Ghetto." *New York Times*, November 12, 2006. Available online. URL: http://query.nytimes.com/gst/fullpage.html?res=9B02EFDB113FF931A25752C1A9609C8B63&sec=&spon=&pagewanted=4.

Daily Mail (London). "As Palin Sees the Funny Side; The Real Deal: Sarah Palin, The Comic Fake: Tina Fey," *Daily Mail*, October 20, 2008.

Dargis, Manohla. "Learning on the Job about Birthing Babies." *New York Times*, April 25, 2008. Available online. URL: http://www.nytimes.com/2008/04/25/movies/25baby.html.

Dowd, Maureen. "What Tina Wants." *Vanity Fair*, January 2009. Available online. URL: http://www.vanityfair.com/magazine/2009/01/tina_fey200901.

Dunn, Jancee. "Tina Fey: Funny Girl." *Reader's Digest*, April 2008. Available online. URL: http://www.rd.com/your-america-inspiring-people-and-stories/tina-fey-interview/article54446.html.

Dwyer, Jim. "Getting in Palin's Hair, or Close to It." *New York Times*, September 16, 2008. Available online. URL: http://www.nytimes.com/2008/09/17/nyregion/17about.html?.

Falcone, Lauren Beckham. "Comedy Heavyweight Fey Shed Pounds, Gained Success." *Boston Herald*, December 4, 2008.

Franklin, Nancy. "Sketchy Comedy: Tina Fey's *30 Rock*." *New Yorker*, December 8, 2008. Available online. URL:

http://www.newyorker.com/arts/critics/television/2008/
12/08/081208crte_television_franklin.

Gay, Jason. "Meet Four-Eyed New Sex Symbol, 'Weekend
Update' Anchor Tina Fey." *New York Observer*, March 4,
2001.

Goldman, Andrew. "Interview with Katherine Pope." *Elle*,
October 28, 2009.

Gorov, Lynda. "With New Comedy, Fey Gets 'Mean.'"
Boston Globe, April 25, 2004.

Guest appearance. *Late Show with David Letterman*, October 17, 2008.

Heffernan, Virginia. "Anchor Woman: Tina Fey Rewrites
Late-night Comedy." *New Yorker*, November 3, 2003.
Available online. URL: http://www.newyorker.com/
archive/2003/11/031103fa_fact?.

Hiltbrand, David. "A 'Grounded' Tina Fey Expands Her
Territory to Movies." *Philadelphia Inquirer*, April 28,
2004.

Hitchens, Christopher. "Why Women Aren't Funny."
Vanity Fair, January 2007. Available online. URL: http://
www.vanityfair.com/culture/features/2007/01/
hitchens200701.

Huffington Post. "Tina Fey's Emmy Night: Humble,
Wants to Stop Playing Sarah Palin." September 22,
2008, http://www.huffingtonpost.com/2008/09/22/tina-
feys-emmy-night.

ImprovOlympic. "Interview with Jason Chin." Available
online. URL: http://users.ren.com/improv/www.
improvolym.com/shows/improvst.

Itzkoff, Dave. "Please Don't Tell Her She's Funny for
a Girl." *New York Times*, March 18, 2007. Available

online. URL: http://www.nytimes.com/2007/03/18/arts/
television/18dave.html.

———. "The All Too Ready for Prime Time Players."
New York Times, January 2, 2005. Available online. URL:
http://www.nytimes.com/2005/01/02/arts/television/
02dave.html.

Jacobs, A.J. "Tina Fey, Make Us Laugh." *Esquire*, May 1,
2008. Available online. URL: http://www.esquire.com/
women/tina-fey-0508?click=main_sr.

Jevens, Darel. "Returning for an I-Opening Look Back:
Stars Reminisce About Their Alma Mater on Its 25th—
er, 24th—Anniversary." *Chicago Sun-Times*, August 21,
2005.

———. "They're Everywoman: Roles Multiply as Improv
Gets More Female-friendly." *Chicago Sun-Times*, April 6,
1997.

Johnson, Steve. "Colbert, Fey and Carell: Comedy's
Power Players." *Chicago Tribune*, December 6, 2009.

Kohen, Yael. "We'll Show You Who's Funny." *Marie
Claire*, April 1, 2009.

Kurtz, Howard. "Online, Sarah Palin Has Unkind Words
for the Press." *Washington Post*, January 9, 2009.

"MonkeySee." "*SNL's* Michaela Watkins 'Just Too Classically Pretty to be Hilarious'?" September 9, 2009.
Available online. URL: http://www.npr.org/blogs/
monkeysee/2009/09/snls_michaela_watkins_just_too.html.

Naanes, Marlene. "Tina Fey Shaping Sarah Palin's Image
on *Saturday Night Live*." *amNewYork*, October 9, 2008.

Notable Biographies. "Tina Fey Biography: A Happy-Go-
Lucky Nerd." Available online. URL: http://www.
notablebiographies.com/news/Ca-Ge/Fey-Tina.html.

Oprah.com. "Tina Fey's Aha! Moment." From the June 2003 issue of *O, The Oprah Moment.*

Pearlman, Cindy. "Fey: Even if *30 Rock* Fails, It's Still a Win-win Situation." *Chicago Sun-Times*, October 8, 2006.

Perigard, Mark A. "Lemon Aid: Tina Fey Hoping Palin Impersonation Will Boost *30 Rock*." *Boston Herald*, October 26, 2008.

Poniewozik, James. "Palin vs. 'Palin': When *SNL* Parody Becomes Campaign Reality." *Time*, October 9, 2008. Available online. URL: http://www.time.com/time/printout/0,8816,1848735,00.html.

PTI, The Press Trust of India, Ltd. "Fey Denies Being Mean to Sarah Palin on TV Show." December 2, 2008.

Russo, Dan. "Tina Fey Returns Home for Deadline." *News of Delaware County*, April 4, 2004.

Ryan, Maureen. "Tina Fey's Climb to the Top of the Comedy Heap." *Chicago Tribune*, September 30, 2007. Available online. URL: http://archives.chicagotribune.com/2007/sep30/entertainment/chi-0930_tinasep30.

Ryzik, Melena. "The Guide on the Laugh Track." *New York Times*, October 30, 2009. Available online. URL: http://www.nytimes.com/2009/11/01/arts/television/01mele.html.

Sanneh, Kelefa. "Laughing Matters: Saturday Night Politics." *New Yorker*, October 27, 2008. Available online. URL: http://www.newyorker.com/arts/critics/television/2008/10/27/081027crte_television_sanneh.

Saturday Night Live, "Tina Fey Plays Palin in Katie Couric Interview Parody." *The Nation*, September 28,

2008. Available online. URL: http://www.thenation.com/doc/20081013/fey_video.

"Second City Alums Remember Their Roots." *Chicago Sun-Times*, December 12, 2009.

Senior, Jennifer. "Funny Girl: *Saturday Night Live*'s Tina Fey Finds Laughs in High School Cruelty." *Daily Breeze*, April 30, 2004.

Session Magazine. "Tina Fey American Writer." December 5, 2008. Available online. URL: http://www.sessionmagazine.com/tina-fey-american-writer.

Simonini, Ross. "The Sitcom Digresses." *New York Times*, November 21, 2008. Available online. URL: http://www.nytimes.com/2008/11/23/magazine/23wwln-comedy-t.html.

Smith, Kyle. "Leap of Fey." *People*, May 3, 2004. Available online. URL: http://www.people.com/people/archive/article/0,,20149986,00.html.

Spitznagel, Eric. "Tina Fey." *The Believer*, November 2003. Available online. URL: http://www.believermag.com/issues/200311/?read=interview_fey.

———. "Tina Fey: Playboy Interview." *Playboy*, January 2008. Available online. URL: http://www.playboy.com/articles/tina-fey-interview/.

Stanley, Alessandra. "Still Biting the Hand that Feeds." *New York Times*, October 14, 2009. Available online. URL: http://www.nytimes.com/2009/10/15/arts/television/15rock.html.

———. "Who Says Women Aren't Funny?" *Vanity Fair*, April 2008.

Stein, Joel. "Goddess of the Geeks." *Time*, April 26, 2004. Available online. URL: http://www.time.com/time/magazine/article/0,9171,993922,00.html.

Thomas, Mike. "Laugh Lessons: What Today's Top Comics Learned at Second City." *Chicago Sun-Times*, September 27, 2009. Available online. URL: http://www.suntimes.com/entertainment/books/1790574,SHO-Sunday-unscripted27main.article.

"Tina Fey Gets the Last Laugh." *New York Post*, April 25, 2004. Available online. URL: http://www.foxnews.com/story/0,2933,118079,00.html.

West, Kelly. "Interview: Tina Fey Talks about *30 Rock*, (Part 1)." Cinemablend, April 1, 2008. Available online. URL: http://cinemablend.com/television/Interview-Tina-Fey-Talks-About-30-Rock-Part-1-9723.html.

———. "Interview: Tina Fey Talks about *30 Rock*, (Part 2)." Cinemablend, April 1, 2008. Available online. URL: http://www.cinemablend.com/television/Interview-Tina-Fey-Talks-About-30-Rock-Part-2-9724.html.

Winfrey, Oprah. "Oprah Talks to Tina Fey." *O, The Oprah Magazine*, January 2009. Available online. URL: http://www.oprah.com/world/Oprah-Winfrey-Interviews-Tina-Fey.

Witchel, Alex. "Laughing When It Hurts: *Saturday Night Live* Anchor Tina Fey Struggles While Making Comedy out of Tragedy." *New York Times*, January 21, 2002.

Zimbio. "Sarah Palin Pokes Fun at Herself at Journalists' Dinner." December 6, 2009. Available online. URL: http://www.zimbio.com/sarah+palin/articles/c9Ne4F-HqpML.

Zuckerman, Ed. "A Professionally Funny Family." *New York Times Magazine*, November 24, 2009.

INTERVIEWS

Author interview with Harry Dietzler, December 9, 2009.

Author interview with Professor Douglas Grissom, October 13, 2009.

Author interview with Jane Morris, November 17, 2009.

Author interview with Jeff Rogers, December 17, 2009.

Author interview with Professor Richard Warner, October 18, 2009.

FURTHER RESOURCES

WEB SITES

The Internet Movie Database, Tina Fey
  http://www.imdb.com/name/nm0275486/

The Second City
  http://www.secondcity.com

Tina-Fey.org
  http://www.Tina-Fey.org

INDEX

PICTURE CREDITS

ABOUT THE AUTHOR

JANET HUBBARD-BROWN, a graduate of New York University and author of many books for teens, has spent months immersed in the life of Tina Fey, watching videos, reading every article she could get her hands on, and studying the world of improvisation and sketch comedy. At the same time her daughter, Ramsey Brown—for whom Tina Fey is a major inspiration—has been navigating her way through the Los Angeles world of funny women writing and presenting their own material. Hubbard-Brown is particularly grateful to the entertaining interviewees in this book.